Adventures from the Last Century

Adventures from the Last Century

a memoir

Carl Craven

ANGELINA
RIVER
PRESS

This is a memoir; no names of people or places have been changed.

ISBN: 978-0-9883844-0-8
Library of Congress Control Number: 2012954566

Manufactured in the United States of America

Angelina River Press, LLC
Fort Worth, Texas

Acknowledgments

My brother Jerry really made this book a reality. Thanks for his encouragement and hours of work with the manuscript.

Special thanks to my Sister Sue for the hours she spent proof-reading. It did not matter to her that she was recovering from a broken pelvis at the same time. I cannot thank her enough.

Charley Ritchie touched my heart the two summers I worked for him. He was a perfectionist who was allergic to people especially when they tried to direct him. Charlie was a great friend. I still find it hard to keep a dry eye when I remember him.

Doctor David Silberman my family doctor suggested I take Omega 3 when we found my body would not tolerate statins. He mentioned that such fish oil often comes from menhaden. That triggered my memories of the menhaden fishing trip; I thank David for reminding me about the menhaden boat and for keeping me healthy.

Special thanks to the Cajun student I called "The Great White Hunter." Before school every day he put on his hip boots, took his 410 shotgun and other weapons and waded in the swamps behind his home to run his spring-loaded traps, hoping for trapped varmints his family could eat. I thank him for sharing his captured live albino opossum (a creature with large, ugly teeth) with the entire West Orange Middle School one fine day in the early sixties. His hunting to help feed his family reminded me of my dad when he was a boy hunting in South Texas.

for Patricia Craven

CONTENTS

Scam Date 1958

I rarely dated in 1958 mostly because I was very shy and was a starving college student. She was very good looking. She asked me to take her to a church social box lunch dinner on Saturday night. You know, one where the guys bid on the gal's box dinner, and the money all goes to help support the church. Then the two of you go somewhere quiet and share the meal she had prepared with loving care.

Did I mention that she was really good looking? I was flattered and needed no prompting to accept. I picked her up her parent's home at the prescribed time and took her to the church. She was hyper and laughed loudly and talked much without really saying anything.

It was a big church, and she knew everyone. She took me around and introduced me to everyone we walked by. Then she asked me to drive my car some distance and pick something up that she needed. It was a long drive but she was eager, and I wanted to please her so I went on this fool's errand.

When I got back to the church all the boxes had been auctioned off except hers. A deacon was with her, and they were

1

really glad to see me. He was an older man, probably in his thirties, with a pencil thin black mustache and wore an expensive looking dark suit. She introduced me to the deacon, and with a vigorous handshake he welcomed me to the church almost as if I had joined or was about to make a lifetime commitment. He then told me that they needed just ten more dollars to make the total church donations amount to five hundred dollars.

I obliged his open hand with my last ten bucks. It was the sum total of my emergency funds, but I figured it was going for a good cause. The beauty was thrilled and almost jumped up and down with joy as she gave me a paper sack with her name on it. I peeked in with some disappointment at two peanut butter and jelly sandwiches. Then before the deacon could walk away, a man on the public address system said he was pleased to announce that the total church donations for this wonderful event amounted to just over eight hundred dollars.

The lying deacon still had my money in his hand. He vanished fast, presumably to add to the total the man on the public address system was talking about. I later wondered if the lying deacon was also a thief. Did my last ten bucks really go to support him or the church?

At that point the beauty told me that my errand was one she and her boyfriend had made up and that he was going to take her home, so it would be best if I left immediately. I gave her back the sack of sandwiches and departed feeling very used. I never saw her again.

I rarely dated back then because I was a shy, starving college student. Did I also mention that I was gullible? About a year later I saw in the paper that she had married a deacon in the church. The picture in the paper showed an older man in his thirties with a pencil thin black mustache and wearing a dark, expensive-looking suit. For ten bucks I will tell you the name of the church.

For another ten I will try to remember her name.

Postscript: This was the only date I ever had where I picked up a girl at her parents' home and never returned her. The parents must not have been too upset; they never called asking about their daughter. Better yet they never called my parents wanting to know where we were "at this ungodly hour," something that happened a few years later with another extremely good looking woman. But that is another story I may never tell.

Breakfast by Carlson

Oscar Irving Carlson liked to fry up a couple of pounds of bacon into crisp sticks. He melted out all the lard he could get from the bacon. The result was a cast iron skillet loaded with hot grease. He then set two slices of bread in the skillet frying them until all the grease soaked into the bread or it could not hold any more lard and the bread slices turned black and heavy. He would then put the Pan Blackened bread on a plate, put about a quarter of a stick of margarine, on the bread, covered it with black strap molasses, and proclaim it French toast.

He liked to cut a bite size chunk of margarine with a fork, stir it around in the molasses, and eat it. Always he smacked his lips and offered to share with anyone still in the room. I tried to leave before he took the first bite of Oleo.

I don't remember his ever getting any takers, so he ate the two slices of bread, all of the bacon, and at least one stick of oleo—all covered with copious amounts of black strap molasses.

When Oscar was in his early seventies the family doctor diagnosed him as having the worst case of arteriolosclerosis he had ever seen. I suppose that if Oscar had eaten better and had not smoked several cartons of Pall Mall cigarettes a week, he might have lived to 99 as did his brothers. He lived to be 77 in spite of his alcoholism. Supposedly his death was due to complications of hernia surgery he had about six months before his demise. There may have been a few other contributing factors. Perhaps it finally all caught up to him.

Hungry Tom

Parenting 101 is a game I play. I earn points for adding a curriculum item to this imaginary class—one that should be mandatory for prospective parents. It should be required prior to inception, an impossibility, I know, but I still get one point per agenda item.

The new item must evoke at least one emotion (fear, hate, love etc.) and needs to be true. I earn extra points for extra emotional entanglements and extra points for the item being intuitively obvious even though you or your parent failed the lesson. Keep in mind that strong sexual passion totally blocks out intuition and items that are otherwise obvious. Let me give a few simple examples.

The year was 1970. It was the second or third Saturday morning of January, give or take a few hours. The wife asked me to get down a twelve pack package of toilet paper from the top shelf in the hall linen closet. The top shelf was too high to reach. While wife and thirty-seven-month-old son watched, I jumped up and swatted at the package a couple of times. It finally budged. It fell to the floor. My son said, "That son of a bitch." Wife and I did a sudden gasping inhale. She said, "We don't talk like that in this house."

The son's prompt response was, "Daddy does."

I could not remember talking like that around my son but it was embarrassingly obvious that I had been caught. I knew at that moment of the need for Parenting 101.

Two of my agenda items:

Never change a new baby's diaper on your own bed at 2:00AM. The yellow volcano eruptions may not have subsided. This can seriously damage your bed sheets and drive you crazy due to lack of sleep.

Remember that what happened in the heat of passion on a Sunday afternoon may require you to teach a child how to drive a car in about sixteen years.

Agenda items can grow and multiply faster than redneck jokes and can have a real impact on your life and future needs for counseling or therapy.

Most people are not born with much intuition, and common sense is not at all common. We as parents do the best with the tools we have at the time. This is why every future parent should be required to take Parenting 101. The savings in counseling sessions alone could pay for the class.

I often hear agenda items on radio and TV. Some common repeats are:

—Never leave your child in the back seat of your car with the engine running while you hop into a convenience store for a pack of smokes.

—Never leave your toddler alone near a swimming pool.

I met Tom one day when I was fifteen. If anyone ever needed Parenting 101 it was his parents. He was my age, but he was taller. My brother Jerry and I met him when we visited the family of a man Dad worked with. Tom and his parents lived in a small house near a large group of warehouses.

An odd thing we noticed in the house was the padlock bolted onto their refrigerator. My mother was shocked and asked about the lock. She was thinking that theft must be rampant in this poor neighborhood. Tom's Mom said that she had to have the lock to keep Tom from eating everything in their refrigerator.

Tom had been outside and entered the kitchen about then, and he asked if we wanted to go out and play, which we did. He took us to a fence beside one of the warehouses and told us to watch him find something good to eat.

We stood outside as he climbed over a chain link fence with barbed wire across the top and entered the building through a broken window. Inside, he broke open a box and filled his pockets with small packets of jelly like you get in restaurants. When he climbed back over the fence, he ate the contents of about a dozen of the jellies.

Brother and I declined the eat any of his stolen goodies. That much pure jelly seemed like a pretty disgusting thing to eat. Besides, we were not as hungry as Tom. He told us that he was hungry all the time, and that he had discovered he could always find a meal in one of the food storage warehouses.

The next day Mom quizzed us about the incident. It seems

that the police had called her after an investigation, that Tom admitted to taking the jelly. Mom wanted to make sure we had not participated in the theft. When she was assured we had not taken or even eaten any of the stolen jelly she called the police back to tell them about that padlock on the refrigerator.

We learned later that when they saw the lock on the refrigerator the police contacted some other authorities who took Tom away from his parents. We never saw any of them again.

Mom and Dad's house rule on food while we were growing up was simple. If we had food in the house it was fair game for anyone to eat at anytime. Anyone included family, friends or even strangers that came knocking on the door on a cold night looking for help. That rule never changed. It is now my rule in my home.

Parenting 101 agenda items I learned from the meeting with Tom and his family:

If your child is thin, hungry often, and eating you out of house and home, run to the nearest store and buy more food.

Never ever put food in your home under lock and key.

Spit and Polish

Dad often repeated an old saying about polish and excrement, something Hank and Betsy heard but ignored.

Hank, a rude, crude and abrasive kind of a guy was an amateur rock hound and spent a lot of time playing with hard rocks and fossils. He learned that the igneous rocks could be put in an old tire with some sand and turned on rollers for days. This would produce shiny rocks that looked like marbles. While not perfectly round they were highly polished and shiny. People liked them and he could sell them on the internet for a small profit.

This was an easy way of avoiding human interaction.

He found an old sea bed in Texas that was abundant with fossil shark poop. He put several coprolites in the old tire and turned the electric motor on low spin. After a few days he opened it up only to find they had completely dissolved.

Hank proved that Dad was right: you cannot polish a turd.

Betsy had a thing for Hank. She loved him in her own way so she moved in with him, but her way was very controlling. She wanted to change some (most) of Hank's habits since he was crude, rude and abrasive to almost everyone. So their relating was often difficult.

Hank was not totally at fault in the turbulent relationship. Betsy wanted total control of most things in her life. Sometimes her approach lacked the finesse that could have allowed her controlling techniques to succeed.

Take her horse as an example. She gave her total attention most Saturdays to training the horse, to correcting its behavior. One Saturday it responded by stepping on her foot. Because this horses was very heavy and wore iron shoes, the simple step broke several of Betsy's bones and left a hell of a bruise. Weeks later while still peeved over the beat-up foot she tried to reprimand the horse. The horse took offense again and bit her hip hard enough to require several stitches and a patch in her blue jeans. More weeks passed and she tried a more serious reprimand to change her horse's behavior. She goaded it along with spurs and a quirt. The horse leaned against the fence and walked along it, dragging Betsy's leg against the fence until it had scraped much the skin from her leg and broke a bone in the leg. She obviously knew little about training a horse.

Betsy wasn't doing any better with Hank. She tried several similar wrong rough ways to change poor old Hank. The first time he laughed and made fun of her until she cried. The second time he punched her out. This left her with a black eye to go with the aches and pains from the horse. Hank promised her more of the same only worse if she kept it up. She sold the horse and moved out of Hank's house.

Betsy had finally realized that Dad spoke the truth. You cannot polish a turd.

Car Care

In 1953 Dad bought a 1942 Buick, a large car. The entire family fit in it with comfort. Dad applied his usual car maintenance rules to this Buick:

—add gas as needed

—never bother changing the oil

Sometimes he might check the oil, but only if he was going on a trip of several hundred miles. Such maintenance worked well for over two years. When the check oil light came on it was too late, for something really bad had happened to the engine.

Dad decided to fix it because that was his nature. The engine would not turn over at all, and he thought it might just need a new piston. He took out the right size box wrench to remove the bolts the held the head on. The bolts did not want to turn at all, so he took two-foot length of steel pipe as a cheater and slipped it over the Craftsman wrench. The bolts would still not budge. Not to be deterred, he used a five-foot length of steel pipe, and by putting most of his two hundred sixty pound behind this lever, the bolts finally turned. The box wrench twisted to a forty-five degree angle from the handle but didn't break during the removal of the bolts.

The Buick needed more than a new piston. It needed a new short block with pistons and valves, which would cost more than the $300 dad paid for the car. So Dad had the old junker hauled away. He replaced it with a 1947 Kaiser for $300 cash.

One Saturday I went with dad to the automotive tools area in Sears. He handed the bent Craftsman wrench to the clerk. He looked at it and walked over to a bin, picked up a brand new wrench of the same size and handed it to dad. Dad put it in his pocket and we left. No one even asked how the wrench got bent. I was sure someone would ask, then void the guarantee, but no one did.

Dad treated the Kaiser as he had the Buick. He added gasoline when it ran out or got real low. He probably checked the oil some but not often. When the 1947 Kaiser rolled over 118,000 miles, it died as had the Buick. Dad did not even try to fix it. We shoved it to the end of the driveway where it was not in the way, and Dad bought another $300 car.

Daddy Pop wanted to sell the Kaiser, which Dad had declared to be worthless and told him to go ahead, that he could keep any money he got for it.

Daddy Pop put a $3 ad in the paper, and the first day the ad ran someone came by and paid Daddy Pop $35 for the privilege of hauling the Kaiser away. That was more money than he received in a month from Social Security, so Daddy Pop was thrilled and gloated for days.

He bought several cartons of Pall Mall cigarettes, a couple of pounds of thick-sliced bacon and a tin of black strap molasses.

The price Dad would pay for a car seemed to be $300. This went on every two or three years for over a decade. He was skilled a picking the cars. If the seller asked a lot more, Dad, with Mom beside him, haggled for a long time. His clincher was to pull out $300 in wadded up dirty fives, tens and a few twenties he had put together just for that occasion. He would declare it was all the money he had in the world and that he did not work steady enough to qualify for a loan. If that was not enough money to buy the car he would have to go to a different dealer. The ploy generally worked.

Sometimes the wadded-up bills came to only $290. Then mom offered her "last ten dollars" to seal the deal. She produced a wadded up old ten from a raggedy change purse that had nothing else in it.

I never saw such bargaining fail. We never drove a new car, and we never had car payments.

The House with Glass Windows

The Family as of 1949

Oscar Irving Carlson   Mom's Daddy   AKA Daddy Pop

Daddy Pop lived with us most of my life. He remarried just before we went to Venezuela, but he played a major role in the family.

Mom called him Daddy and dad called him Pop. When mom and dad got in an argument mom would yell for Daddy to take her side and dad would yell for Pop to take his. We heard Daddy followed by Pop so often that Sue and I started calling him Daddy Pop. His role as an arbitrator was frequent and never easy.

Gorman Andrew Craven: Dad

A dreamer, our Dad, a wonderful man, missed Parenting 101. I learned to be an absentee father by his example. Dad could build anything with his hands. If it had never been done before he would be given a set of plans in a dream, then he would build it.

Charlotte Rosebell Craven:Mom   AKA Bell (later Bell Meek and AKA G. G.)

An early equal rights woman who could not be suppressed. She was a great mother and never cleaned our house when she could get someone else to do it. She took advantage of the equal rights at the telephone company. She more than tripled her hourly earnings by moving from telephone operator to a position that had always been done by men. One test she had to pass was to climb creosote covered wooden telephone pole with spikes to the top and back down without getting hurt. She did it the first try. One of her women friends slipped and slid down the pole. Doctors removed the splinters in the emergency room.

Carolyn Susan Craven: Big Sister   AKA Susan King
Did you ever meet a person that read all the books of a home edition of the Encyclopedia *Britannica* before the age of thirteen? She is now a widow, mother, grandmother, college English teacher, cancer survivor and wonderful Older Sister.

Carl Andrew Craven: Me   AKA Big Foot
I also missed the freshman class called Parenting 101. Like Dad I did the best that I knew at the time. My shoe size grew over the years. At 15 I wore a size 12. At 30 I wore a size 13. At 60 I grew to a size 14.

Gerald Allen Craven: Little brother AKA Doctor Jerry Craven
When he was a senior in high school he told me he hated Math

and Engineering. He vowed that he would have doctorate in English before he was 30. Mission accomplished at age 29. What foresight and determination.

Gail Laverne Craven: Little sister   AKA Doctor Gail Fail
Gail joined us in San Tomé, Venezuela. She is now a wife, mother, grandmother, Botanist, college teacher, and the best little sister in the world.

The Adventure Begins

Our Great Adventure actually began before we knew it. It started in early 1946 when Dad caught the mumps from his children. They were really hard on him. As the saying goes "They went down on him." It was not a two weeks and you're well mumps case. He was swollen up like he was carrying two cantaloupes. It put him out of commission for about six months. He could not get up and walk around without pain. Because he rarely got sick and was not a good patient, he became depressed and irritable.

In an attempt to cheer him up, Mom found some job opportunities in South America, ones that paid high salaries and had tax advantages for living in a foreign country. It did cheer him up enough to fill out several applications. He then got well and went back to work.

He had almost forgotten the applications when he got a great offer from a company in Venezuela. All he had to do was respond and pass a physical. Excitement filled the air around our house. He took and passed the physical and answered all the oil company's questions properly. By November 1946 he was in Venezuela. Company housing for the rest of the family was supposed to be available in about six months.

The Family Trip Begins

The promised housing was delayed, so he rented a house in a native village and arranged for us to move to Venezuela. We moved a lot when we were kids, though a trip to Venezuela to join Dad was more exciting than moving to Galveston. This would be our biggest trip ever. I was nine. I asked mom when she was in her eighties if she remembered the date we left for Venezuela. She said she remembered only that brother Jerry turned six the first week we were in Venezuela.

We boarded a train that left Corpus Christi at midnight, probably on the last Saturday night of March, 1947. We awoke in Houston, left the train and boarded a bus early Sunday morning and found ourselves on and off busses for the next 24 or so hours, arriving in Miami Beach, Florida before noon on Monday.

We spent Monday night in a very old large hotel somewhere in Miami Beach. The next morning we had a nice pancake breakfast at the hotel, our last meal on American soil for four and a half years. We then took a taxi to the airport and flew to Havana, Cuba.

The Havana airport was a small building in the middle of a grass field—not solid grass like a golf course but scrappy with scattered clumps of grass among patches of dirt. Airport officials made us wait for our next plane outside the Airport building in and around a bar closed to children, even for bathroom breaks.

Tables with umbrellas and chairs provided the only shade around, so we sat down to get out of the sun. A waiter popped out of the bar to tell Mom she had to order drinks for us to make use of the chairs and the umbrellas. She ordered four cokes.

The 1947 price of a Coke was a nickel in Texas. The Havana Cuba price was a dollar each plus tip. Our Pan-American plane finally arrived barely in time because we were still not allowed to use the bathroom in the bar, and the Cokes were working their way through the system. An airport official informed us that the plane would have the only restroom we could use. After some people got off and a crew cleaned up the area, we were finally boarded and got rid of the Cokes.

The stewardess gave us several small boxes of Chiclet gum. Instead of the usual ten pieces of gum we could buy for a nickel we got these small boxes free. They gave us extra because we thanked them politely for the gum. Some of these small boxes had two normal sized gums and some contained a single double sized candy coated gum. We each got a pocket full of the small boxes. They said we should chew the gum to help our ears adjust to the changing altitude. I was not impressed with our visit to Cuba but the Pan-Am Stewardesses were great.

We arrived at the Caracas airport in surprisingly quick time. I had not even chewed up all the gum. We saved the empty boxes for the used gum. Stewardesses collected our trash before we landed. They gave the rest of a bowl of gum to the three of us kids. We left the plane much happier than we had been during our stay in Cuba.

We found Dad and changed planes. The new plane was more of a small transport plane than a passenger plane. It belonged to the oil company. The seats were filled with boxes and plants, so the pilot had to clear off enough seats for us. He put the cargo on the floor and in the aisles and directed us to not touch it. Most of the cargo was cactus and other thorny plants, so we found it easy to obey him. Since we had no stewardess to give us gum or drinks, I dug into my pockets and found gum for all of us. It was a short flight to the small San Tomé airport.

The First Rental House

Dad took us on a quick tour of the oil company camp called San Tomé. He showed us many beautiful homes and the Country Club we belonged to as employees. We had never even seen a Country Club before. Then he drove us to our new rental home in El Tigrito.

The white house was the last house on the road at the edge of town. It was made of cinder blocks set on a concrete slab.

Later we discovered that we would not use the front door. Dad always parked the pickup around back, and everything we ever needed was in the back.

There were no screens on the doors or windows. The back door had once been an over-sized door that had been cut down with a hand saw to cover the opening, mostly. It did not have a door knob. The outside had a hasp for a padlock, and the inside had a large wooden bolt sort of like what might be used in ancient castle. From the inside you could lock everyone out and from the outside you could lock everyone in.

The door had a two inch gap at the bottom where rats, large centipedes and other varmints could just walk in whenever they wanted. I know. I saw them do it. I chased out the ones I saw but others slipped by me, and Mom usually found them. We could tell she found something ugly because she usually screamed. Like when a centipede wrapped itself around her wrist three times. She shook it off with a hard fling of her wrist. Every place a centipede's leg scratched her became infected. Her wrist looked like they all scratched her.

I stepped in the back door that first day in our new home. To the right was a kitchen work counter, but the room had no shelves, drawers, doors or drapes. The counter top and floor around it was covered with boxes, buckets and wash tubs full of dishes, groceries and other household goods, evidence that Dad had spent days shopping for us.

Just beyond the kitchen was a dining table and chairs. When I looked up, I found the metal frame that held the corrugated metal roof. Light leaked in around the eaves of the roof, and I could tell that insects and small birds found their way into the house around the eaves.

The house had a total of three rooms. From the back door I could see two bedrooms on the left. The bedrooms were about ten feet by ten feet. The kitchen /dining room took up the rest of the square house. Then I looked hard at the window next to the table. It was decorated only with steel bars—no drapes, shades or screens. Dad said the bars were to keep people out. You could stick your hand outside between the bars.

The house had no utilities as we knew them. A kerosene lantern provided all the light available at night. The kitchen stove was a Coleman camper stove. Water came from the rain barrel that caught run-off from the roof, and we had to carry water inside. Plumbing was a privy out back. So we had no toilet to flush and no bathtub except for a number three galvanized tub. We found that by using our biggest pot and the camper stove, we could have all the hot water you could produce, which wasn't much. Trash collection consisted of our carrying garbage to a deep hole in the back yard. As it filled or became too smelly Dad tossed some gasoline in followed by a lit match. Sometimes it took a second match to ignite the gasoline.

Mom was afraid we would fall into the garbage pit when making a night journey to the privy. The garbage pit was deeper than we were tall. She gave us each a flashlight—though it was only for night time privy use. We could not play with our flashlights because we would drain the batteries.

Brother and I quickly learned how simple it was to just pee on the ground. It did not matter whether it was night or day. We usually tried to get away from the house but the urgency of the mission did not always allow for this. We soon discovered it was best if Mom did not see us, though Dad never said anything when he saw us. He peed on the ground, too, when Mom was not around.

It's a small wonder that Mom's first question to Dad after seeing the house was "When is the next plane home?"

Dad tried to cheer mom up. He pointed out that most of the native homes were made of mud with dirt floors and palm thatch roofs where scorpions could fall on people at any time. Many had no door to close and no windows with or without bars. The chickens, pigs and other animals wandered in and out of the house when they wanted. Mom was not cheered.

We drove by many of these thatch and mud homes. Often we saw a woman sweeping the dirt floor with a straw broom. This still puzzles me. We always swept the floor to remove the dirt. But why sweep a dirt floor? How would they ever know when to quit? No matter how much they swept there was more dirt.

The children's beds were metal framed army cots with two inch thick cotton mattresses. Each bed came with a small stuffed cotton pillow. I wanted to use a hammock as the natives did. The house came with hammock hooks in every room, but had no hammocks. We did buy one later. It made a good swing but I did not like trying to sleep in it. We loved to play with the cotton filled pillows. Since there was no ceiling we made a game of tossing the pillows from room to room over the walls. We tried to hit whoever was in the other room. We lodged a pillow in the metal rafters a couple of times, and it was my job to get it down using a chair and a broom handle. It was a simple task for me since I was the tallest. When a pillow hit mom by mistake she put a stop to this game.

When it did not rain enough to fill the water barrel, we purchased water from one of the local water trucks that delivered river water. Sometimes this water contained river minnows that we seined out and pretended that they had not been in our water supply. The men selling the water were amazed that we worried about minnows. They knew that if the minnows were alive the water had to be fresh and good enough to drink. After all it had not killed the fish.

After a while brother and I did drink this river water, though it took us a while of watching the locals drink it. One day I was really thirsty and in a hurry, so I drank right out of the barrel. It tasted good and did not make me sick like Mom said it would. I had seen locals drink the water, and it had not killed them off.

The first morning in our new house Dad heard the boys making normal hungry sounds. He opened a can of powdered milk, showed us how to mix the milk with water, and dug out some dry cereal, sugar, bowls and spoons from the boxes in the kitchen area. I sat at the breakfast table eating a bowl of corn flakes when a donkey just outside the window started. Loud. The noise almost jarred me out of my chair and woke up everyone else in the house. Jerry and I jumped to the window and peered out between the bars. The burro had poked his head over a barbed wire fence and was screaming his lungs out inches away from our window. I had not known that burros could be that loud. After everyone was up and had seen the burro Dad chased it off.

Sue decided she was hungry, so I found her a bowl and spoon. A few minutes later she asked why the black spots in the milk were moving around. The dry cereal we had just opened was crawling alive with bugs. Sue called them weevils. Jerry and I had already eaten half a bowl of the infested cereal. Sue was amazed we had not seen them moving around. She wisely refused to eat the cereal. Dad opened the other boxes of cereal, but the bugs had found all of them. So we had fried eggs for the rest of breakfast.

Dad cooked them on the Coleman camper stove. He had already filled it with fuel, so he only had to pump it up and light it. He opened a fresh can of Crisco lard for cooking oil. Mom said the lard was stale. Dad said he had just opened it. Jerry and I got the first two eggs. We ate them up not caring how fresh the oil was and went outside to play before the argument got serious.

Mom was quite upset with the house. She kept nagging Dad to tell her when she could catch a plane for the States. We kids just took it in stride. We probably did not know any better but we looked at having the house as another adventure, and we knew we would move again soon. We just had to wait and it would happen. The next house could not be worse. We always moved. It was what we did. But Mom was ready to leave immediately and proved quite vocal about it.

It did not make her feel better when Dad told us that it was a lot better place to live in than the tent his Dad had moved his family into when Dad was fourteen. For years when we drove around and saw a dilapidated old shack, Mom asked Dad if that was our next home. I doubt that she ever totally forgave him.

The Itinerants

I finished the fourth grade in San Tomé, Venezuela. It was the fifth different school I had attended. I had gone to one school twice but with a gap of about a year. Sue said the one word that best described our family was itinerant. For years I thought that the word applied only to migrant farm workers. Dad followed construction work, so I just knew itinerant did not apply to us. We knew we were not gypsies, hobos, or vagabonds even if we did travel from place to place with no consistent home. It's funny how you can get the wrong sense about words based on how they are used on the radio and in the newspaper. But Sue was right: like it or not, we were itinerant.

Before we left Texas we stocked up on clothes because we were told Venezuelans did not have clothing stores. Somehow we believed this lie. Even though they did not dress most of the young children until they puberty, all the adults wore some clothes, and all parents seemed to have some Sunday clothes for their children. We found many clothing stores, often owned by Arabian families. We became friends with some of them. We even found a Sears store in Puerto La Cruz.

The Legal Differences

Everybody knows about their culture's laws. We learn them in from our parents and in history lessons. In our country we know we are presumed innocent until proven otherwise. Most of us believe our laws are good and are fair and that Laws are based on common sense.

Then what happens if you move to Venezuela? The heritage is different. The culture is different. Then you learn that laws do not have to be good, or fair, or logical or based on common sense. Everyone knows what common sense is. You don't have to possess any but you can recognize it. Then perhaps when you are older you learn that most people don't have a speck of common sense, that common sense is not common. Many laws seem so clear and black-or-white: if you run a stop sign, you break the law. I thought I knew the law, though I was nine and living in Venezuela. But how wrong I was.

Mom and Dad warned us that the laws in Venezuela were based on arcane Spanish laws and not knowing them could get you in trouble. For example, in Venezuela if you were accused of a crime, you were automatically presumed guilty until you proved yourself innocent. Sometimes you had to do the proving while in jail. Another tough law they told us about appeared to contradict the automatically guilty law. If you accused a Venezuelan of stealing and did not have three credible eye-witnesses, defined as adult Venezuelan nationals, they could sue the stuffing out of you for defamation of character.

At first I thought it was designed to protect the poor from the rich and was to the benefit of the thieves, but later I began to suspect this was only part of it. It kept the North Americans somewhat in check, but the real reason for the law seemed to be that it came from Venezuelan cultural beliefs.

Perhaps the law about accusing without witnesses was based on reactions to the brutally cruel dictator Gomez. He was a barely literate sheep herder who became a general, then a dictator who ruled Venezuela from 1908 until his death in 1935. The brutalities he inflicted on the people of Venezuela were monstrous: during his reign people lost hands for stealing or for just the accusation of theft. An old cultural belief became law under Gomez, one concerning lopping off the left hand of a thief, then right hand for another infraction, and then the head. The irony is that Gomez was likely a thief himself: though born a sheep herder, he died the richest man in the country.

Current laws as we saw them in Venezuela appeared to be the pendulum swinging the other way after the dictator's death. At best the laws were confusing, illogical, and to us lacked any semblance of common sense. I decided to stay away from thieves and laws. Since I had never even seen a thief, staying away from them was not going to be much of an imposition. I wouldn't know a thief if I saw one. But it still worried me some. I discussed it with Dad and he told me that there were two kinds of people, the caught and the uncaught, folk wisdom that every kid in the world probably heard while growing up.

At nine such "wisdom" seemed mean and intentionally confusing, so I decided to stay away from thieves, laws and Dad's old sayings. But, alas, all were unavoidable. Dad would say things like: "If the dog hadn't stopped to pee he would have caught the rabbit" or "Every little bit helps said the little old lady as she peed in the ocean" or "You can get used to anything even shit it your hat." He seemed to have a wise saying for every occasion, and never mind that they often contradicted each other.

Whistling Frogs

We arrived at the start of the rainy season, a time on the high plains when rain fell every day around three in the afternoon. You could almost set your clock when it started raining, and you could see the rain coming across the field. It rained hard for a while and left a lot of standing water to play in. After the first rain the whistling frogs appeared and started to serenade us. They were amazingly loud and whistled most of the night. Within a few days the puddles were loaded with tadpoles as the frog cycle went on. The whistling was almost nonstop.

My brother and I got pretty good at imitating the whistle. Some nights when the whistling slowed down a bit we would beat the frogs up into a whistling frenzy with our fake frog whistle. This aggravated Mom and Dad when they caught us encouraging a frog serenade. They encouraged us to not do this with threats of violence upon our rear ends. We had to limit our whistling at the frogs to daytime and even then we could whistle only when we were away from the house. It was fun and gave us a sense of power over the breeding frogs.

A Pink Dress

We drove by the same store almost every day where a beautiful girl about two years old played in the sandy dirt in front of the store. The thing that really made her stand out to us was her clothes. She always wore the same thing: golden stud pierced earrings and two small pink ribbons one on each side of her head. She always played in the mixture of sand and specks of asphalt along the side of the road. For toys she had an old tin can with the top cut out and a dirty tablespoon. She filled the can with the tablespoon and dumped it out. It seemed to entertain her for hours.

Mom was itching to take her picture but worried that her parents would take offense. One day she had Dad stop and we all went into the small store that belonged to her parents. Dad explained the obvious—that we were North Americans. He went on to say that we saw their beautiful daughter every day and would like to have their permission to take some pictures of her. They were delighted.

They whisked the girl into another room. In a short time they brought her out all washed. She had on a beautiful pink dress, a pair of pink socks, pink shoes, a pink bonnet and long white gloves. I thought at the time that they could not find pink ones. They had replaced the golden stud earrings with what appeared to be about one carat diamond studs. It was a magical transformation. Mom was amazed that they owned that amount of clothes for her and tried not to show her disappointment. But she rose to the occasion by taking pictures of everyone holding the girl until she ran out of film. We thanked the store owner and his wife for the honor of taking the photos. Mom promised them copies as soon as we got them developed.

A few days later we drove by with more film and took some shots of the girl in her normal state of dress. Mom snapped the shots from the pickup window. We all stayed in the truck and drove away before we were noticed. When the original film was developed mom had two copies of each shot printed. We stopped and made a big show of giving them a complete set of the pictures. Mom had everyone review each photo. The girl's parents were thrilled.

Mom developed the other film later and sent most of the shots to relatives in Texas. Sue may still have a photo or two that were left in Mom's carved chest. I forget the girl's name.

Our First Military Road Block

We drove from El Tigrito to San Tomé nightly to fill up a large water can with shaved ice and drinking water for the next day. We had been in the country for a few weeks when on one of these treks we were stopped in our first military police road block set up by the bridge to the El Tigre River. The Army in Venezuela was also the national police force. I never found out why we were stopped that night, but they stopped all traffic in both directions. If they had a reason for stopping everyone they never gave it. But then again they were the national police and did not have to explain their actions. They were stopping and inspecting all vehicles then letting them go. They ordered Dad to get out of the pickup. They frisked him and confiscated his pocketknife. Dad was really pissed when the police captain took his favorite Barlow out of Dad's pocket. The chief inspected it and apparently liked it, so he dropped into his own pocket.

The captain asked Dad to open the tool boxes in the back of the pickup, a request that worried Dad because a work crew had left a dozen machetes in the toolboxes. If the police confiscated his pocketknife, what were they going to do to him for having a dozen sword-like weapons in his truck? The boxes were not locked so Dad just opened them. Using powerful flashlights they merely glanced at the machetes and ignored them.

Dad was more than miffed when he asked with all the politeness he could muster why they took his small pocket knife and ignored the large machetes. He explained that to his way of thinking the machetes were far more dangerous. The police captain looked at him like he was a child and told him he thought just like a North American. The machetes were tools needed by men to earn a living while the pocketknife was a concealed weapon that could be used in a surprise murderous assault. He then ordered Dad to drive on. By the time we returned with our iced drinking water the road block was gone.

We learned that the maximum legal size for the open blade of a pocket knife was two centimeters. A longer blade made it a concealed weapon. Dad bought each of us one of these tiny pocket knives. They were terrible. While the handles were pretty with bright colors, you could not throw such knives and make them stick into anything. A game of Mumble Peg was out of the question. They were too dull even to cut kite string. The metal in the blade was such poor quality it would not sharpen no matter how you tried. You could scratch up the chromium coated blade, but the metal under that was not capable of holding an edge. The end of the blade was so blunt and thick it did not even work to scrape dirt from under finger nails. The only thing my brother and I could do with them was to lose them. So we did.

It may have been illegal to carry a regular sized pocketknife, but it was not illegal to sell them, so Dad purchased another one. A new Barlow cost him about three times as much as he had paid for the confiscated Barlow in Six Points Hardware in Corpus Christi, Texas. He kept the new one under the dashboard of the pickup, and he took it out only when there were no police in sight.

The Great Dove Hunt

Dad's best friend invited him to go dove hunting, though we kids knew it was really Dad's idea. The invite was just a ruse to get Mom to agree. She said it would be okay if he took both the boys, so we prepared to go dove hunting. Dad and his friend hand-loaded two boxes of shells for their shotguns. We had sling shots. We carefully picked out pockets full of the best round rocks we could find in our gravel driveway.

It was a couple of hours drive to a dove migratory path, but we did not care how long it took for we were going dove hunting with Dad. Actually Jerry and I had never been on any kind of hunting trip. We had been fishing a lot but never hunting. We had heard so many fun hunting stories from Dad that we were eager to grab some of the fun.

A few hours north we came to an area where doves by the thousands were flying across the road. Dad said this is it, the dove migratory path used every year by thousands of flocks of doves. We drove a way off the paved road, and Dad parked behind a large clump of trees to conceal the pickup, and we got out, prepared for the slaughter. In just minutes the first flock came flying by. Jerry and I shot rocks in the air and missed them all. Dad and his friend fired in the air and knocked down a bunch of them. Our slingshots were no competition for the shotguns.

Dad had us pick up the birds. Some were just stunned and started to fly away. Dad yelled at us to grab them and wring their necks. We learned the best technique for wringing bird's necks, but we never liked it. Soon we were so busy picking up the dead and wringing necks we did not have time to shoot at the doves. New flocks just kept on coming. When Dad and his friend ran out of shotgun shells birds kept on flying over. By then we had gathered up over fifty doves so our hands were bloody from wringing all those necks. We were tired and did not want to shoot one more dove.

Then came to the part we liked even less than wringing necks. We had to help remove the feathers and clean them. All fifty had to be cleaned. Our sling shots had killed zero but we got to share in the cleaning. Fortunately Dad was exceptionally quick at cleaning birds. He could pluck and clean about ten birds to our one. Dad was even faster than his friend.

It appeared to me that his friend liked the shooting best, and that he was happy Dad was so good at the cleaning chore. Dad's friend picked at the job in about the same slow pace we did. He then filled a large water can with doves and covered them with shaved ice. When it was full we discarded the remaining birds. Dad's friend said that they would spoil before we got them home. We washed our hands with soap, water and dry rags Dad had brought just for that purpose. It had never felt so good to have clean hands.

We got home happy enough and listened to Dad and his friend brag about a successful hunting trip. He told mom how good the boys were and how they had helped with everything. I did not think we were that good, but we had helped with everything but the shooting. I did not want to ever wring another dove's neck (and I haven't).

Dad got out two huge skillets and a second Coleman camper stove and set them on the ground in the back yard. In each skillet Mom stirred up a batch of brown gravy made from lard. It took one stove per skillet. She then cooked up about fifty doves, a time-consuming process on the small stoves. When the birds were finally cooked, we were famished.

The best part of the day was the feast. I do not remember how many doves each of us ate but there were no leftovers. The entire meal consisted of several loaves of bread, gravy and doves. We all got our fill of the small tasty doves. It was a great hunt.

The Law and DDT

Bugs got into everything, even things that seemed to be sealed. Canisters with flour or sugar, boxes of cereal (open or not) would often have small wiggly things in them when we opened them. This was despite the fact that every house in Venezuela was sprayed with DDT twice a year. They often mixed the DDT with a white paint base and sprayed every wall inside and out of the house. This is why many houses were white.

The army had a group that came around and sprayed all houses, huts and shacks. They then stenciled DDT and the current date on the front of the house so they could tell when it had been sprayed. If anyone painted over the stencil they would come back and spray the house again and put up a new stencil. They maintained a six months schedule.

We always left the house for the day when they sprayed. Dad usually talked them out of using the white pigment when spraying our house. This pigment kept the DDT residue on the wall permanently. We also threw out any food that was not canned. Despite this the weevils, centipedes and other unwanted varmints found their way in the house and in our food. This may have had something to with mom rounding us up every year and giving us a powerful vermifuge. We had to swallow this poison to kill the worms we probably had and then we took a powerful purgative to get the poison and dead worms out of out of our body before either could harm us. It was about as much fun as preparing for a colonoscopy.

Big Brother

Growing up as a big brother was often difficult. When younger brother was six I was nine. I was about a foot taller and strong enough to pick him up and carry him away from trouble. I rarely did this because it really made him mad. He would yell, hit, kick and bite until I put him down. I was sure I could have overpowered him in an emergency but that was not my job. My job was to keep him from being hurt and out of trouble, not to fight with him. Every time we went out to play mom would tell me my job. "Don't let your brother get hurt and keep him out of trouble." That was clear enough. I guess it never occurred to her that both of us could have been hurt or found trouble without really seeking it out. I only knew I was not going to start any trouble. It certainly never occurred to me that anything in the world was bad enough to hurt either of us. I was nine. Besides we lived in the safe, small town of El Tigrito, Venezuela. What could hurt us there?

I took Jerry with me on many "Let's get out of the house and go exploring" trips. Sometimes it was my idea to go out but often he would tell me it was time to go exploring, for we both loved these outings. Sometimes we took a local young man named Felix with us. He showed us how to find wild spiny cucumbers, wild guavas, figs and other fruit we could eat. He taught us the good from the bad. You can eat this wild red fruit but not the yellow one that looked similar. He taught us that wild guava often contained white grub worms. You needed to tear the fruit open before eating it. If you only found one or two white grubs it was okay to flick them out with your fingernail, then eat the fruit. If there were a lot of grubs present just toss it and try another guava.

We no doubt ate several guavas with grubs before we knew to look for them. It did not seem to hurt us no matter how awful it sounds to eat a grub worm. Such "food" may have been one reason mom found it necessary to give us a yearly vermifuge. Still, I doubt there were any bad pathogens in the grubs. The Australian Aborigines eat another kind of grub worm all the time without harm. Figs had a similar problem. Many of them contained one ant. Tear open the fig and the ant runs out mad and looking for a fight. Just shake the ant off and the fruit is good to eat. If the fig is full of ants, toss it. There are always plenty of figs on the tree.

After a few of our grazing trips Jerry became better at finding these prizes than I. What an aggravation! He could scurry around and find things faster than I could. At first it really upset me, but I got over it. He eventually went on these explorations without me but not until mom relieved me of the job and duties of his caretaker and protector.

We went on family picnic trips most weekends to see the wonderful sights not to be found back in Texas. One Saturday we went to a small canyon to the south of where we lived. We started out like we were going to the Orinoco River but soon turned right down a dirt road. After about half an hour we came to the canyon. It was huge to us but tiny compared to the Grand Canyon, which none of us had seen, though we had read about the Grand Canyon in the Encyclopedia Britannica.

Dad drove the pickup up to the edge of this canyon. As we approached you could not tell it was a canyon. It looked like we were about to find a river. The horizon had clumps of green trees like when you are going to a river. As we got close you could see some of its cliffs.

We got out of the pickup ready to go exploring. Mom reminded me of my job to watch little brother. That took some of the fun out of exploring. We walked a way around the canyon's edge and found ourselves in an area thick with underbrush taller than I. Just off the trail we could see the walls of the canyon and the edge of the cliff. There were many trees in the bottom of the canyon. They grew a hundred or so feet tall, nearly to the top of the canyon walls.

Suddenly we heard a loud crash as something hit the canyon floor. Mom said, "Where is Jerry?" We all yelled for him but got no answer. My heart sank as guilt surged for not having him by the hand. I ran back toward the pickup yelling for him. Around a couple of bends I found him. He was bent over and looking at some pink flowers on a short bush the rest of us had missed. He asked me to tell him the name of the flower. Sue caught up in time to hear the question. She told him the name of the flower.

She said it was a common plant she had noticed as we got out of the truck and did not deserve any special attention or she would have pointed it out to us. She always knew about plants and flowers. She was still feeling the scare that he had fallen into the canyon, so she scolded him for not keeping up with the rest of us. He ignored her and ran down the trail to Mom and Dad. He was no longer interested in the flower and was not about to listen to a scolding from Sue.

We walked back down the trail and caught up with everyone. Dad said he had figured the crash out. He found a fresh exposure of wet red clay on the canyon wall. He pointed to the large red clay spot on the canyon wall. It looked like someone had used a giant shovel to gouge a hunk of it out of the wall. Just below was a pile of the same red clay on the canyon floor. Dad surmised the noise was just a small incident of mass wasting: part of the canyon wall had eroded away. A recent rain must have loosened up that part of the wall, and it fell to the floor of the canyon with a loud crash. Such erosion must have happened often during the rainy season. We found several other spots of exposed red clay on the canyon wall with splats of red clay on the canyon floor directly below. So we left the top of the canyon to find a safer place to explore.

On a road cut into the canyon, likely by one of the oil companies, we drove down into the canyon to find the river. We did not know the canyon contained a river, though we felt sure it did, and inside the canyon had to be a safer area to explore. At least that was what mom said. We did find a river and other safer places to explore.

Jerry and I were allowed to roam around El Tigrito in very limited scope of our neighborhood. Mom pointed out our boundaries in every direction, ones we soon found to be far too restrictive, so we expanded them to fit our needs without bothering letting Mom know.

We took to walking several miles down to the river, then we headed away from the river and when out of sight of our home, we turned back in a big loop back to another spot on the El Tigre River, which was supposed to have piranhas, electric eels, and a species of small fierce alligator called the baba—all dangerous creatures we had strict orders to avoid.

But we were sure the river did not contain any of those

animals. The locals washed clothes and swam in the river every day. We felt certain that if such beasts lived in the river the locals would not even approach the water, for they were more prone to fear than was Mom. Even our tame pet dogs scared the dickens out of all the natives. So on long hot days we often walked beyond Mom's boundaries to a shallow part of the river to cool off in the water.

Once we walked past three older boys. They decided to follow us and taunt the crazy Americans with foul language. After a while the oldest one ran ahead of us stopped, yelled and dropped his pants. With some pride he waved a huge erect penis. This scared the stuff out of us. I told brother to run for home as fast as he could but he was already ahead of me. They laughed and taunted us as we sped away but did not chase us. We never told anyone of the ugly experience. We avoided the river for a while. When it got hot and we could hear the river calling we found an alternate route. Fortunately we never saw that scummy trio again. Sometimes Mom would quiz us about where we had been. We learned to have a consistent prefabricated story to tell mom to make sure we both told the same lie about where we had been.

One day Mom sent us to the local store for a cooking banana and a can or two of Spam. If Dad was going to eat with us we needed two cans of Spam. In Venezuela there are two main kinds of cooking bananas, the platanos and the topochos. Both are related to the smaller eating banana. They contain less sugar and more starch than eating bananas and are not considered fit to eat raw.

Platanos also means plantains. The topocho is a variety of plantain. It is also another Spanish word for banana. In El Tigrito topocho refers specifically to the fat square shaped cooking banana. The platanos are about a foot long and are round shaped. You know if a plantain is ripe enough to cook when there are as many black spots on the peel as yellow. If the peeling is solid black it is ripe and best if cooked immediately. The topocho can be cooked green, but you have to pound the slices with a mallet meat tenderizer.

To prepare it properly you must pound it, soak it in milk for about an hour, dry it off and pound both sides with the mallet again. The slices were ovals about the size of Spam slices. Mom fried them in the same hot lard as the Spam. If you fried the Spam first, everything tasted like Spam.

Mom used Crisco. It came in cans and was not always stale like some other brands of lard. The pounded topocho did not taste so good, but the platanos were great, often caramelizing in the hot lard, which made them taste sweeter. When the frying was complete Mom added flour, powdered milk and water to the hot lard to make a great tasting grease gravy. She called it cream gravy, but lard was the main ingredient, and I know she never used any cream. If we were out of powdered milk she sometimes used canned condensed milk. It was a meal we had often in Venezuela. We never heard of cholesterol back then. We only knew the diet was good if it filled us up and we did not get sick that night. Fried Spam and fried bananas was always a welcome meal.

As we went to the store Jerry ran ahead of me. A drunk staggered out of a building with no name or markings on it. I had always suspected it was a bar, and upon seeing the drunk I was sure it was a bar. The drunk headed our way, screaming and cursing at us for being criminal Americans, accusing us of robbing his country of its natural resources.

This was silly—we were just young kids. Besides, everyone knew that the oil companies had to pay the Venezuelan Government half of their oil profits. I ran ahead and placed myself between him and Jerry while directing Jerry to get as far away from the drunk as possible. He looked and acted dangerous, especially when he picked up a piece of wood from the middle of the road.

It was mostly shredded from having been run over so much. It looked like it had started out as a two by four, but it fell apart into a dirty shredded stick. He waved the stick at us and screamed that it was his duty to kill us and rid his country of two criminals. I was about to tell Jerry that we had to run for home when the store owner came out carrying a large black walking cane. The cane looked to be hand carved from a two by two piece of black iron wood.

Iron wood is so dense that it will not float in water and is naturally black. Sometimes it has streaks of lighter wood in it. This walking cane was solid black and looked fearsome. The store owner screamed at the drunk to run away or he would beat him to death. The store owner was about twice the size of the drunk and he looked like he was capable of such violence.

The drunk looking scared, dropped his stick and ran back to the bar. He peeked out the door but the grocer yelled and walked toward him in a menacing way waving the black cane and yelling that he would kill him if he caught him. The drunk vanished from sight.

The store owner told us not to worry about the drunk, that the crazy man was just a drunken communist. The store owner said he would watch over us, that he would never let that scum scare off any of his customers. The man calmed us down with a free ice cold orange soda.

Jerry did not appear to be as upset as I. He was mainly interested in the cane. The store owner let us pick it up and hold it. It weighed at least twice as much as I had guessed and was polished as smooth as it was black. A whack to a man's arm would surely break some bones. While Jerry admired the beauty of the ironwood, I saw the pictures at the end of the counter, a shrine-like arrangement of the photographs Mom had taken of the girl in the pink dress. Brother, sister and I were all there with the girl in pink as the center of attention. I suddenly relaxed.

After we had both carefully inspected the carved ironwood, the store owner told us it was the store's protection and peace maker. When he took it out, troublesome people always left. We were pleased with the cold drink and the visit; both calmed me down almost as much as seeing the photos of the girl in pink. We got the food we were after and made it home safely. The store owner followed us most of the way, black cane in hand, just to be sure.

A few days later the store owner told Dad of the incident. I understand that Dad had some people talk the drunk into leaving town forever. At least that is what Dad told me. We never saw that man again, drunk or sober.

The evening meal we brought back proved quite satisfactory. Dad was there, so we used both cans of Spam and two platanos. Many thanks go to the store owner for everything. He sold us the food on credit. He protected us. He gave us a free cold pop—though Dad may have paid for the two ice cold orange sodas when he settled the account balance some weeks later. I hope so. The cold sodas were really good. The comforting and protection the store owner gave us was priceless. We could have been killed, or so I thought at the time.

At some point Mom relieved me of my duty to protect Jerry. After all, we never had been in any real danger, at least none we ever told her about.

Mom had helped protect us from the drunk without knowing it. She made a big deal out of taking the pictures of the store owner's daughter in the pink dress. Dad also protected us without my knowing it at the time. Some years later Mom told us the she was sure Dad had something to do with the demise of a communist agitator who had tried to disrupt his work. I could not believe that. But once it occurred to me that the communist might have been the same drunk man who had threatened to kill his sons with a shredded dirty old stick, I found the story one I could and do believe.

The Mango and Cashew Hunt

We went on a weekend picnic to find some mango trees. Dad wanted to pick some free wild mangos. Going on an outing and picking free fruit sounded like a fun thing to do, for we all loved mangos. Two native friends, including a Mr. Martinez, went with us.

Dad stopped near a river with lots of huge mango trees. As we were walking toward the trees my brother and I spotted a small plant with a bright red fruit. He beat me to it, picked it and ate it. One of the Venezuelans that had come along as a guide saw him eat the fruit. He screamed that the plant was poison. Mom nearly went into hysterics. She told me later that she had been convinced that her six-year-old boy had just eaten a deadly poisonous plant in a foreign country and was going to die.

She grabbed brother and tried to force her fingers down his throat to induce vomiting. In the process she inflicted a cut on his gums with her fingernail. Brother, truly angry was resisting as hard as he could. He screamed and kicked. His bleeding from the fingernail cut made the scene more tense. He screamed as loud as possible, given that Mom was trying to poke her fingers down his throat. Jerry was trying to keep his teeth clenched.

I ran over and told Mom that the fruit was not poisonous. We had eaten dozens of these plants ever since Felix had taught us they were good to eat. Vastly relieved, Mom put Jerry down, and he walked around kicking the ground, spitting and cursing under his breath. He did this for quite a while, muttering that his scratched gum really hurt.

He found another red fruit. This time he gave it to Dad. After some discussion Dad cut the fruit into pieces with his new pocketknife. He smelled and tasted it, then said it looked, smelled and tasted like a similar red fruit he had eaten in the Rio Grande valley when he was growing up in Texas. We all had a small piece of the red fruit. It was really tasteless. We moved on to the mango trees. That is except for Jerry and Mr. Martinez, who still proclaimed the fruit to be poisonous, and he was sure we would all get sick and die. Brother remained behind, cursing under his breath and continuing to dislodge small clumps of grass by kicking the ground.

The mango trees were enormous. The limbs near the ground were higher than we could reach and were more than a meter in diameter. We could see some green mangos well over 100 feet from the ground. The other man who came with us on the trip started to climb to the first limb, which proved a mistake because suddenly some howler monkeys showed up.

They screamed and threw monkey poop at us. We were not about to climb any tree that tall full of large screaming monkeys throwing crap at us. They knew we were after their food and let us know we were not welcome to it. We decided that the mangos we could see were all green anyway, a decision that reminded me of the old sour grapes story. The adults wisely determined that we would simply have to get our mangos at the local market and pay for them.

So we walked around and found some cashew trees. The fruit looks like a small red pear with a large nut on the bottom. Inside a husky shell is the actual edible part of the nut.

Dad taught us that you have to roast the nut to get the toxic juices out of it. The pear-shaped fruit can be eaten but most people are allergic to the fruit and—like Mom—break out in ulcers when they touch it. We tasted it and did not like it, but Mom was stuck with ulcers in her mouth for several days. My brother and I ate the fruit with no after effects beyond a bitter taste that went away.

The pear-shaped fruit turned from green to yellow to red in various combinations as it ripened into a bright red. The almost ripe fruit, red with some yellow, tasted horrible. The fully ripe fruit was bright red and was only fair. None of the stages of the fruit were particularly good. Some of the indigenous animals like deer and capybara eat the fruit—and they are most welcome to all of it. We did not even gather any of the nuts for roasting.

More than once, I watched the preparation of cashew nuts. My friends built a wood fire encircled by rocks ten to twelve inches in diameter. They put a flat piece of tin on the rocks over the fire and loaded it up with cashews in their husks. During the roasting someone shook the tin, gripping it with a pair of pliers or a cloth. When the cashews were properly roasted, they beat the husks away with a large spoon and put the nut meat into a bowl. When the bowl had enough cashews in it they would break the nuts into pieces and ground them up with the same spoon.

They wiped off a section of the hot tin with a dirty looking wet rag and roasted the cashew bits until they were a powdery brown. Then they mixed the powdered nuts in a fifty-fifty ratio with sugar—sometimes white sugar, but most of the time they used cheaper brown sugar. They continued cooking the sugared nuts on the hot tin, taking care not to burn or melt the sugar. The final result was a sweet powdery mixture. It was a bit dry but very sweet.

We ate it like candy and ignored the grit from left over husks and dirt. Being addicted to sweets of any kind, I loved it. The process was probably not all that sanitary, but Mom was never at our friends' house when they cooked the sugared nuts, and we always ate it up in a few minutes. I never made the recipe at home—but then we didn't own a piece of dirty flat tin, and building a fire in the back yard was not an option Mom would have tolerated.

I still remember the trouble my brother and cousin Andy got in at the age of three. They lit a fire under our house to roast some marshmallows. Mom put the fire out, then spanked the boys and yelled at them considerably. In our Venezuelan yard, it was bad enough when we had to burn the trash pit. Mom supervised that very closely when Dad was not around to start the burn.

The House with Glass Windows

We moved into the second house shortly after the great dove hunt. It was a bit larger and was unique in that it was the only house in the entire village of El Tigrito with glass windows. It still had bars in the windows in case someone decided to break the glass. The windows opened outwards in levels by turning a crank. We usually kept the bedroom windows open for fresh air.

Dad often looked for anything to make points with Mom. He even installed an inside commode in the storage room off the patio. We could flush it by pouring a bucket of water in the tank and then pulling the lever, or we could just pour the water in the bowl. Mom was happier when we left it flushed, filled the tank again, and left the seat down. We always tried to flush it but sometimes we forgot to refill the tank. This was a known way to rile Mom. Sometimes we intentionally neglected to flush, but generally we simply forgot. Sometimes we were in a hurry to go out and play.

The shower was an old zinc milk bucket with a valve and a shower head soldered in the bottom. It was set on a block wall about shoulder high in the room next to the commode, and the shower had a real drain. We had to fill its tank with water and turn on the valve to take a shower. Heating the water on the stove was optional. Mom and Sue always wanted hot water but I did not mind the water right out of the rain barrel. The kitchen had a real sink. You still had to carry water to it, but to empty it you just pulled out the stopper.

I do not know where the milk bucket came from. We never saw any fresh milk the entire time we were in Venezuela. If there were any dairies around, we never saw or smelled one. The lack or electricity in the country would have made it difficult to keep milk refrigerated. All our milk was powdered. We usually bought milk in a one-gallon can size except when we were short of money.

The best powdered milk was an expensive Danish brand. When you mixed it up and let it sit for a while cream would rise to the top. It was much like real milk, only better, for we always used more powdered milk than recommended to get better taste and produce more cream. I liked to sprinkle powdered milk over my corn flakes and then add sugar and water. This way I did not have to mix the milk first. I only had to stir it up once. If I did not get the milk mixed up enough I would get a mouth full of powdered milk. This would suck all the moisture out of my mouth. A sip of water corrected that and I would resume eating. The powered milk by itself tasted really good to me, so I learned to take small amounts in my mouth at once.

Mom especially loved the cream. She mixed it fifty-fifty with her coffee and then added a load of sugar. Likely I got my sweet tooth from her.

The Danish brand of powdered milk was even better when we could chill it in the refrigerator, an appliance we had when we lived in San Tomé. The oil company Dad worked for provided the refrigerator and the required electricity to run it.

But most of the time we spent in Venezuela we did not have a refrigerator. We did not even have an old fashioned icebox that needs a new block of ice regularly—we had one of those back in Texas.

But leftover food was a rarity in Venezuela, so we didn't much miss having a refrigerator. One-dish meals were common, and what we did not finish at mealtime we fed to our watchdogs.

Our house with glass windows had screen doors and real doors with door knobs. They fit the door opening and did not let varmints in. The roof was the same—corrugated zinc—and there was no ceiling. A big difference from our more primitive house was the eaves were sealed, so bugs and birds could not get in. It was a bigger and nicer house. The garbage pit in the back yard was not as deep. There was a dry well and a water tower in the backyard. But we still did not have running water or electricity.

We had moved again by January. On my tenth birthday we lived in San Tomé. This was a real, North American style house with inside plumbing and electricity. The oil company furnished it completely. While it was wonderful, with only two bedrooms, it was a bit small for our needs. Then in San Tomé, the house of all houses (for us) became vacant. It was a four-bedroom three-bath home. The fourth bedroom with bath was clearly for a maid. Mom immediately named it the maid's quarters, so that had to be its function. We had hot and cold running water, inside plumbing, electricity, a refrigerator, and a large kitchen stove with an oven, a large pantry, and wonderful furniture—all provided by the oil company for a small fee. It was a really beautiful home. While growing up we never had a better house.

The First Rosa

Mom finally realized one of her lifelong dreams. She got a maid. It seemed mandatory. The house came with a maid's quarters. It also made Mom as happy as we had ever seen her.

It seemed strange that the maid did not live with us. Instead, she used the maid's quarters as a home base on the days she worked, and she kept the room filled with clothes to be washed and ironed.

The maid rode the bus back and forth from El Tigrito, and we paid the bus fare in addition to her wage. Her job seemed simple enough to define, but the workload was enough to kill a mule. All she had to do was the laundry, cook two meals a day for the five of us, mop the floors and do any other chores Mom wanted.

She and her two babies could eat the same food we ate if they liked it—but they could not stand North American food. Rosa got weekends off. The three of us kids had been doing the maid's chores for as long as I could remember and we never got weekends off. Saturdays we got to go to the movies but we never had the weekend off. Still, we were happy to relinquish the chores to Rosa during the week. Mom was overjoyed.

Rosa was a young local girl barely past thirteen. She already had two babies and, as often happened with women in her position, by two different fathers. She had never been married but no one was surprised or even cared. The real problem was that she did not know how to do most of the chores asked of her. She had never seen a house with running water, inside plumbing, a clothes washer and drier, or a kitchen stove that did not burn wood. She could not cook American food. Mom felt the girl could learn with a little training, so we hired her anyway.

Mom told her to do the laundry once a week, and she did. On the laundry day she wrapped the dirty clothes up in a bed sheet and hopped a local bus to the El Tigre River. There she beat the dirt out of the clothes using river rocks and brown lye soap. She sun dried the clothes on the cleanest bushes she could find along the riverbank. Other women used the same bushes over and over again. She picked out some of the twigs, folded the clothes and brought them back on the afternoon bus. She did all this while caring for her two small babies, one of them still nursing. She really worked her ass off on the laundry alone.

My cotton pullover shirts always seemed to be a magnet for the bushes. I got to be pretty good at picking out the burrs and stickers before putting on one of the freshly laundered shirts.

On laundry days Rosa just seemed to vanish. Mom had assumed she would use the washer and dryer in the house, but Rosa had no idea what these machines were much less how to operate them. She used up the bus fare that was kept in a kitchen cabinet drawer at what seemed an alarming rate.

Then there was the problem with our clothes. The two-year's supply we had brought over from the States was wearing out. Mom had hoped we would outgrow them before they wore out, but this was not happening. The quality of the clothes, Mom decided, was just not what she had expected when she bought them.

Often while my brother and I were learning to play tops, marbles and fly kites, Mom spent some time trying to locate Rosa. Finally, Mom asked us to help her keep track of Rosa. When we watched her carry a bundle of laundry and her two babies to the bus we thought she was going to steal our clothes. We discussed confronting her with the theft. I mentioned the possibility of a defamation of character entanglement and that we should be very careful.

But Rosa came back on the afternoon bus with the laundry all beaten clean, dried and neatly folded with some twigs in the same bed sheet. My shirts had the usual quota of thorns and stickers. The laundry mystery and missing maid was solved—along with the source of the twigs and stickers in my shirts. A few days and several family meetings later, Mom simply told Rosa that we could not afford a maid, gave her two week's severance pay and sent her away.

I was not sorry to see her go. Some of the scratchy things never came out of my shirts and she was not learning to cook American food.

Tops for Fun

My brother and I got pretty good at tops, ones we made ourselves from some of the local tree limbs. We cut them branches with a machete, carved the tops from them, then smoothed and shaped them with glass from broken bottles. The top points came from nails we shaped with a file Dad gave us. We learned to string around our tops and throw them to the ground to spin them, and we learned to pick up the spinning tops and hold them in the palm of our hand. We then learned how to spin and catch them in the air without the top ever touching the ground.

Once we saw a boy too young to be in the first grade spin a top in the air and catch it on his thumbnail. He did it time after time without missing—sometimes he even caught it left-handed. He was so good it was disgusting. I practiced real hard a while but my patience and hand eye coordination did not cooperate. My brother practiced until he could catch the point of the top on his thumbnail several times in a row. By then he had a very sore thumb from all the misses that hit the soft tissue near the thumbnail. That's when we moved on to kites and marbles.

Rosa Number Two (Petra)

The second maid started out great. Mom called her Rosa, which was not her name. After our first maid, Mom called every maid Rosa. Sister Sue tells me our second maid's real name was Petra. Anyway she knew how to use the clothes washer and drier, and best of all she could cook North American food. It turned out that she had been the maid for another family that had lived in the same house. We all loved her, especially Mom now that she was sick all of the time. She was pregnant with our new little sister.

More maid trouble was quick to find us. The pantry kept going bare. Only a few days after stocking up it with a truckload of groceries from the commissary it was empty again. One day I went to the pantry for something to eat and only found a gallon jar of Kosher Dill pickles. I found Mom and told her we had nothing to eat. She led me to the pantry to show me where we kept the food in this wonderful new home. Before I could remind her that I was the main pantry stock boy we were staring at some empty shelves. Even the jar of pickles had disappeared in the last few minutes. We really were out of food.

It turned out that our second wonderful maid was not only stealing our food, she was taking our clothes (except for my scratchy shirts) and anything else she could carry home on the bus. The electric iron and the ironing board were on that list. The electric iron was a really weird item for her to take, given that she had no electricity in her home to power it and the ironing board was rather large to carry on the bus. Most of the irons the locals used were molded out of cast iron. They were really heavy and had to be heated on a stove or a wood fire. I understand that it was a real trick to hold the hot handle and keep the ironing surface clean at the same time.

We were paying a maid to steal from us. I had never expected the first thief I was to know in person would be a short, skinny, old woman. A worst shock was realizing our wonderful maid was a thief. In dealing with a thief, the strange foreign laws loomed forth again.

A few days later and after the usual family meetings, Mom intercepted her on the way to the bus. I was with Mom by special request. I was not sure why because Mom had total control of the situation. I had thought that Mom would have me carry back the last sack of the stolen goods, but that did not happen. Rosa (Petra) had a large sack about half her height full of our stuff she was stealing. One of our best bath towels was on the top to hide the rest. She looked surprised when we approached her. Mom told her in the best Spanish I ever heard Mom speak that she could keep the load of loot she was carrying but we could no longer afford her as a maid. Mom must have rehearsed the speech for hours with Dad. She had it down pat. Mom gave her the usual two week's severance pay right there and told her not to ever come back. Petra got on the bus and rode away with the last loot she would get from us. No accusations. No defamation of character. No maid.

We did see Petra-Rose for several more months; when we

did, she was always with another North American woman at the commissary. Rose-Petra worked as a maid for this American woman. Mom never mentioned the problem we had with Petra to the other American woman, and Mom listened politely while the maid's new employer told Mom what a wonderful employee Petra was. Mom agreed with her and never told her that she had hired a thief. I got the impression Mom did not really like the other American woman. Mom told me later that some people just had to learn things for themselves.

Rosa Number Three (Dolores)

The pregnancy made Mom so ill she could do little besides throw up, so we quickly hired the third Rosa. Her real name was Dolores but Mom still called her Rosa most of the time. She could not clean or cook American food. She didn't know how to do any of the chores we expected of her, but she did not steal, and this was a real big plus. Mom tried to take the time to teach her how to do most of the chores the North American way.

Dolores returned the favor and taught Mom how to cook wonderful Venezuelan food. When we left San Tomé and moved to a native village Dolores often went to the local market and returned with some wonderful local fare to cook for us. I thought it was good self-defense on Dolores's part. She did not like our brand of American food (Spam fried in lard) and she was great at cooking delicious Venezuelan dishes. We all loved Rosa, even our new little sister.

Mom and Dad must have made up for a while but she still never missed a chance to needle Dad. Any time we passed a trashy old house, even after we left Venezuela, she always asked Dad if that was to be our next home.

Little sister's arrival was the best thing that ever happened to us in Venezuela. We all took turns caring for her when she was tiny. Even Dad did his share of the diaper duty, and it was a rare day indeed when he did any chores at home. When she got older she would say things in a mixture of English and Spanish. For bread and butter she would say "pan y butter" using the shortest word in either language to convey her meaning clearly. I never thought that mantequilla, Spanish for butter, was easy, and pan is definitely shorter than bread.

The Sandpaper Tree

Dolores even tried to help with the budget. When Mom showed her how to clean dirty pots with steel wool she was amazed that we spent money to buy steel wool. She introduced Mom to the chaparro tree. It grew wild so it was free. The leaves were like sandpaper and could be used to scour pots and pans. The leaves were not as durable as steel wool, but they were free and abundant. When they wore out you just tossed them and plucked some more. You could sand the paint off a truck with these leaves. Mom did use them from time to time when we ran out of steel wool.

My brother and I already knew about the chaparro tree.

Felix had taught us it was a great tree to climb. We climbed one for the first time the second day we were in Venezuela. The trees have soft thick bark. An injury to the tree causes it to produce a lot of sticky resin. Some big black ants that did not sting or bite seemed always to be in the trees. I think they liked the resin. The resin would get all over our hands and clothes, but the climb was worth it. We never told Mom that we sometimes chewed the resin. It was a free gum but a lot stickier and the flavoring was missing. The small white flowers were pretty but smelled really awful. Never sniff them even if you have a chance to. Once we even made a chaparro Christmas tree. It was the only green tree we could find. We painted the leaves bright colors and decorated it like a real Christmas tree. We even found our presents under it on Christmas morning so it must have worked.

A Speed Trap

Most weekends were fun picnic trip days. Mom and Dad decided that we should see as much of Venezuela as possible while we were there. We loaded the pickup with food and water, hopped in the pickup and went off to see something new. It was a great way to have fun.

One Sunday we went to see the city of Cantaura. We may have been heading somewhere else but this was as far as we got. This beautiful small city is tucked into the mountains towards the coast from El Tigrito, about half a mile off the main road.

You had to turn to the right to get there. It was at this intersection that we were stopped for speeding. Everyone was stopped to be inspected and fined. It was the usual run of the mill speed trap. These traps were set up when the police needed revenue. They simply stopped and fined everyone for speeding. The national speed limit in 1947 was thirty kilometers per hour, and everyone drove faster than that. Besides, you were guilty until you proved yourself innocent. If you did not have the fine money they kept your driver's license until you brought the cash in. If you did not have a driver's license they just put you in jail until the fine was paid.

Since very little traffic actually went into Cantaura they moved the roadblock down to intersection with the main road. We were caught like tourists. American speeders were fined more than locals because the police knew that all Americans were rich. This was not really true but on a comparative scale we had a lot more than most of the locals. Paying the fine seemed routine, but the process became more complex. They tried to find other ways to extract additional fines while they had you captured in their net.

We stopped in a long line of vehicles. Dad got out and talked to the police. They quickly frisked him but that trick did not work twice. His pocketknife was tucked safely under the dash board. A young soldier with a loaded WWI vintage .30-06 rifle started calculating the age of Dad's driver's license. He said it was expired and demanded another fine. The license had to be renewed annually. Dad had only been in the country for eleven months so he knew it was not expired. In fluent Spanish Dad tried to explain this to the soldier but to no avail. Dad finally told the soldier that if he wanted to count past ten he would have to take off at least one of his boots.

This is when the soldier turned red faced and pointed his loaded rifle at Dad's belly. It was a scary moment. Dad quickly stopped talking and was suddenly very submissive. That was not like him at all, but he knew that he had crossed the line with the soldier. He also knew that if the soldier accidentally discharged his rifle it would kill him, and the authorities would do nothing to the soldier. He marched Dad up the hill to jail. I was wondering what would happen next when Mom told us she was going to get Dad. She told us to stay in the pickup until she returned. She told us we had water to drink and food to eat and that under no condition should we get out of the pickup, that she would be back soon.

She took her purse and walked up the hill to the police station. No one tried to stop her. It took a while but she came back with Dad. They had a different policeman escorting them. Later she told us she had bribed the chief of police. He had insisted on the armed guard escort to keep Dad from being shot by the angry soldier he had insulted. The guard escort came at a mandatory extra fee payable in cash to the Chief of Police. The bribes were not being shared—the chief of police kept them. He said he would rule on the age of the driver's license in a few days when Dad came back to retrieve it. The escort directed us to turn around and to go back the direction we came from and to not return for at least a week. We were happy to comply. We went home and ate our picnic lunch.

Dad went back for his driver's license and the chief of police was not there. The only police officer there was married to one of the chief's daughters. Dad learned that all confiscated drivers licenses were locked in a large metal desk and the chief trusted no one with the key. Dad went out to his pickup and returned with a large metal screwdriver. He pried open the desk with the son-in-law to the chief saying he could not do that. Just then the desk popped open. Dad started going through a large pile of drivers licenses. He picked out his and several of his friends licenses, then closed the desk so you could not tell it had been opened. He gave the screwdriver to the agitated guard and told him to keep it. Dad told the son-in-law he had just been set up in business. He showed him how to use the screwdriver to open the desk and had him open and close the desk several times without scratching it.

Dad did not have to pay for the driver's licenses he took. It just cost him a large screw driver. When the chief was out of the office, the son-in-law could now collect the fines and keep them. Dad returned his friend's driver's licenses with a smile and no explanation. He told them they owed him a similar future favor he never expected to collect.

Dad had occasion to go with someone else to this police station some months later. The trip was to retrieve the friend's driver's license captured in another speed trap. Dad found the metal desk was broken to pieces, the parts stashed in a corner near the jail cell Dad had been in. The desk had been replaced with a six foot tall locked safe. A clerk in the office explained that the safe now held all important documents like confiscated drivers licenses and that only the chief of police had the combination. They would have to come back later when the chief was there in person.

Dad never saw the son-in-law again. He often wondered if he was still married to the chief's daughter. Dad never went back to that police station to find out. It seemed a bit risky.

Election Day Outing

General elections were held in Venezuela on December 14, 1947. This was the Saturday we had decided to go to Puerto La Cruz to swim in the Caribbean Sea. We were told that this was the first Democratic National Elections Day ever and that it was illegal to travel on national election days. Both were true. The last presidential election held was in 1898, and it was not a democratic election. It was one of many elections by the federal states. We proved that travel on National Election Day is illegal by traveling on that day and being stopped everywhere we went. It took most of the day to get to our destination; it would have been better to have just waited a day.

We left on our Saturday morning adventure despite many warnings. The first policeman stopped us just a few blocks from home. He informed us that travel was illegal, so Dad gave him a small amount of money and he let us pass. We advanced about a mile to the El Tigre river crossing where we encountered a road block. The same captain that had confiscated Dad's pocket knife was there. Dad did his thing with a larger bribe, something the captain accepted, though he warned that we would come to a road block that we would not get by. We drove on anyway and made it through three more road blocks. Dad said had never seen a road block he could not bribe his way past, and we believed him until we came to a fork in the road.

The left fork went to the Capital of the state of Anzoátegui, Barcelona, Venezuela. The right went to Puerto La Cruz, our target destination. The crossroads area looked like a war zone. All traffic had halted, and all engines appeared to be turned off. A large portion of the Venezuelan army appeared to be blocking the road. We saw lots of Army trucks, tanks and several large cannons. Some looked like WWII modern cannons. The one we were parked next to looked like an old cannon that could have been used in the American Civil War. It was clean and looked freshly painted with Venezuelan military emblems. The diameter of the barrel looked to be as big as a professional hard ball. All the cannons seemed ready to fire and were surrounded by soldiers waiting to do just that.

We were stopped and told we could not go anywhere until the election was officially over at 5:00 pm. Dad inquired around and found the officer in charge. He was the highest-ranking officer we had ever seen. We later read in the paper that he was promoted to the rank of General. He bluntly told Dad we could not move until the election was over. It was a warm day and

Dad did not want to have us sit in the pickup for six or more hours but he had been warned that this high-ranking officer could not be bribed. When attempts were made in the past he arrested the people and some were still in jail years later.

We had to wait in the pickup. It had a canvas cover over the back so we were shaded but it was hot. We expected to have to wait a long time so we rolled the canvas side flaps up to let in fresh air and to get a better view. Soldiers allowed Dad to walk around in a limited area, so he wandered about, listening to the soldiers talk.

He overheard a conversation about a change of guard due to be sent to Barcelona. Dad persuaded the unbribable officer to allow us to provide free transportation for the old guard in our pickup. The fresh guards had already arrived. The officer liked Dad's offer and directed a group of soldiers with loaded automatic rifles to climb into the back of the pickup with us kids. The most senior guard got in the front with Mom and Dad.

That was when Dad explained to Mom about his negotiated deal, telling her not to worry about the armed guards, that they would not harm us. The job of the soldier in front was to give Dad directions to the police station and ensure we made no illegal stops.

We drove along a mountain road all the way to the police station in downtown Barcelona. The road was in a sad state of repair with many potholes, but the view was beautiful in spite of the steep cliffs and some hairpin curves.

The chief of police thanked Dad for bringing in the change of guard, then arrested him and had him escorted to jail. By now Mom knew the drill. She took her purse to bail him out, but for the first time she came back without Dad. She walked past us without a word, went down the street to a store and bought a necktie, then returned to the Police Station. This time she came back with Dad wearing the necktie. It was the first time I had ever seen Dad wear a tie, and it was many years before we again saw him in a tie.

Dad had been arrested because he did not have on the mandatory necktie when in the state capitol on a Saturday. Being a foreigner and ignorant of the law was no excuse. He had to stay in jail until he had a tie on; only then could he pay the fine. We thought this was another strange law for a country that allowed children to run around totally nude until puberty.

For an additional fee the chief of police provided a young soldier to escort us until the election was over. We were told that we also had to pay our escort for his time and feed him. He would get us to a beach in Puerto La Cruz by an alternate route. Dad now knew that it was best to keep the young soldiers happy. When the Chief of Police was gone Dad negotiated the escort's fee for the rest of the day. He then gave him about twice that amount in advance.

He was one happy soldier and got us safely through the remaining roadblocks. We made it to Puerto La Cruz and even found a beach where we went wading. The water was beautiful and crystal clear, though by the time we arrived none of us was in the mood for swimming. We were tired and hungry. We shared our picnic lunch with our escort and left the beach.

The election was officially over when we got the happy young soldier to the police station in Puerto La Cruz. He spoke up for us, and we were allowed to leave without paying another bribe or fine. All the roadblocks had been removed, and we went home. Even the fork in the road that earlier had appeared to have half the Venezuelan Army around was devoid of soldiers.

Now that was an exciting and fun filled day, but we could not go on another picnic for a while because the trip had cost so much in bribes. We had to wait until payday before we could go on another fun outing.

We were used to this. It seemed as if we spent half our life waiting for payday to do something. Some things we waited for still have not happened. Paydays never seemed to have enough money, and Mom and Dad never believed in saving for anything.

Rómulo Betancourt was president of Venezuela when we arrived in the country. He came into power by military coup. His first term was from October 19, 1945 to February 17, 1948. He secured half the foreign oil profits for the Venezuelan Government early in his first term. His second six year term started in 1959 when he was elected by direct election.

Rómulo Gallegos was the first democratically elected president of Venezuela. He served from February 17, 1948 to November 24, 1948. A writer/novelist, he was involved in the coup d'état that brought Betancourt into power. Gallegos died April 7, 1969 at the age of 84.

Carlos Delgado Chalbaud ousted the previous President by military coup. He was president of Venezuela from November 24, 1948 until he was assassinated on November 13, 1950 at the age of 41. He was Minister of Defense under President Gallegos, an ideal spot to take control of the country. It did not prevent him from being assassinated.

Germán Suárez Flamerich, who had a PhD in Political Science and Law, was president of the Junta de Gobierno, which meant that he was an interim caretaker or President from November 27, 1950 to December 2, 1952. We left Venezuela around the first of September 1952.

The Blue Skirt Indians

We had heard about the blue skirt Indians so we decided to go see them. This was a small local tribe whose custom was for all the adult men to wear dark blue skirts and the women to wear what Mom called a Mother Hubbard outfit. They made their own clothes using locally grown fibers and dyes. It was easy enough for us to find their small village.

The first one we saw was a man out hunting with a bow and three arrows. They were not made like what you see in North American movies. The bow was made of the local black ironwood that sank in water. It was about five feet long and did not have the shape we think a bow should have. It was straight with the ends tapered from a fatter middle. The string was made of palm fibers woven by hand into string. When it was strung the fiber string was tight, though there was no gap between the string and the bow. The arrows were made of single joints of bamboo five to six feet long and about one centimeter in diameter.

When the hunter shot the arrows, he aimed at the sky. The arrow would go far into the air and then fall straight down on the target. The man demonstrated his skill several times for us. He hit anything we asked him to shoot. Dad bought the bow and three arrows from him. He was reluctant to sell them as he said that it was a lot of work to make new ones, and he needed them to feed his family. When the price got high enough he did part with them. We were going to keep them forever, but they dry rotted and broke in a little over a year.

The Zoo Keeper

One of Dad's friends so loved animals that we thought he should have been a zookeeper. He had a pet vulture for a while because, he said, it reminded him of his boss. Once he left his pair of Scarlet Macaws for a few hours in his Cadillac convertible. When he returned, he found the birds had chewed all the plastic off the steering wheel. The upholstery was also chewed up and covered with bird poop. After that he had a large cage built for them.

He kept a pet baba, a small crocodile, in his shower. His

wife complained that she could not shower so she helped it find the door. Once outside the baba never came back.

He brought home two baby cats someone had given him. Some locals had killed the mother jaguar, and knew he would love the cats, which he kept on leashes until they started hurting him with their powerful playful bites and scratches. He then confined them to cages. He had many cages with wild animals in them.

His wife was never fond of his pets. He awakened her one morning by waving the open mouth of an eight-foot boa constrictor a few inches from her face, then dropped the body of the snake on her chest. When she stopped screaming she divorced him.

We did not see him much after that. Years later while I was in college Mom found a newspaper article telling about his appointment as a zoo director somewhere in California.

Pet Monkey

The absolute worst pet anyone could ever have is a monkey. They are mean filthy animals. They have no shame and when they bite they can take a large chunk out of you. We knew several people with pet monkeys.

One couple kept a Brazilian Marmoset. The small cute little monkey rode around on their shoulders, and it seemed a safe enough pet. But this monkey would bite a chunk out of you in a flash. It also seemed inordinately fond of crapping all over its owners' shoulders. I went into the owner's home once. Once was enough. The monkey lived in the drapes which were full of monkey poop and urine. The entire house smelled terrible.

We knew another family with two boys about my age. They lived in the country near the El Tigre River. The boys were given a pet monkey. It lived in a walk-in cage. These boys teased their pet, making it so mean that it tried to bite anyone who got near it. When the boys approached the cage the monkey screamed and jumped up and down until they left. A favorite trick of theirs was to turn the light in the cage off and remove the light bulb then pretended to be eating something out of the light socket. They left the cage and turned the light switch on. Sometimes it would take a lot of coaxing but the monkey eventually poked his fingers into the light socket and got shocked. Finally the monkey jumped on the boys and bit them anytime they tried to go into the cage, and it would not touch the light socket with any amount of coaxing.

A third friend of mine in San Tomé had a pet monkey about two feet tall. The monkey really belonged to his dad, who kept the monkey chained to a steel post on the back porch. This monkey delighted in catching dogs. He coiled up the long chain and pretended it was real short. He ran back and forth to an imagined end of the chain until a dog fell for the ruse and got too close. The monkey then caught the dog and tried have sex with it. Often when it caught a dog he would hold its ears with its feet to keep the dog from biting and grab the dog's tail with his hands, then poke a finger up the dog's butt. This nearly drove a dog crazy, causing it to yelp and roll around hysterically, but once caught a dog could escape only when the monkey turned it loose. After the sadistic monkey had all the fun it wanted, he let the dog go, then climbed onto the roof and groomed himself as if nothing had happened. A freed dog always ran away yelping like crazy. Dogs that the monkey tortured wanted nothing else to do with that monkey. My friend said that the monkey treated cats the same way. I saw what it did to dogs and had no doubt that a caught cat would suffer the same indignities.

Never get a pet monkey. They are smarter than most people give them credit for.

Dredging Sand

Because Dad was so good at his work the big bosses promoted him, giving him responsibility for all camp maintenance in San Tomé, a city built and owned by the oil company. It provided homes for its employees. San Tomé was two segregated cities called camps. One camp was for North American employees and one for Venezuelans. The North American camp had bigger and better homes with complete landscaping and furniture.

A problem arose with the El Tigre River Water supply for San Tomé. The pumping station had filled up with sand which clogged the pumps so the city could not pump the amount of water needed. Dad dreamed up a solution. He put together a system that would pump water and sand through a four-inch pipe in a substantial stream. The stream would fill up a dump truck with sand in about twenty minutes.

Some of the native just about went crazy over the power of the process. They wanted Dad to take the sand pump to one of the gold and diamond bearing rivers like the Orinoco or Caroní because they were sure the pump could make them all rich. They said that the sand could be run through a big sluice, and that they would work separating out the diamonds and gold for a share of the profits.

Dad was definitely interested so he did some research. He found out that all mineral wealth such as oil, gold and diamonds were owned and controlled by the Venezuelan Government. Landowners had no rights to minerals on their land.

The oil companies paid half their oil profits to the Venezuelan Government for the right to remove and sell the oil. Small wonder so many Venezuelans wanted to be President. Another issue Dad confronted in the notion of pumping such sand was rainy season weather. This is from April to October, a time when the banks of the Orinoco River and its tributary, the Caroní, flood, making pumping sand impossible. What was dry land in February could suddenly be two or three meters under water in April.

A Rare Planning Cycle

As Dad finished his two-year contract with oil company, he realized that he could make a lot more money as an independent contractor. The decision to leave the salaried job left many unanswered questions. Mom and Dad went through a lot of family meetings discussing these problems.

The first problem they discussed was schooling for us kids. We could still attend the oil company provided school, though the cost would be three hundred dollars per month per child, a huge amount of money at the time—and the school fee could go up after a year. With three of us in school, the option was ruled out.

Some of the other North American contractors had school age children, and most of them did home schooling. The most popular was the Calvert Correspondence System, a company that mailed the assignments. The parents saw to it that their children completed the work, then mailed it back for grading. Mom liked the plan, so we went with it. We also ordered a complete set of Encyclopedia Britannica and a World Atlas with maps of all countries in the world.

After Sue read the Encyclopedia a couple of times she had it pretty well memorized. Anytime we needed to reference it we just asked Sue. She just turned to the book and page and there were the answers. Sadly these days the Encyclopedia Britannica no longer publishes hard copy books. It is all computerized now.

Dad determined that he needed a Venezuelan partner, so he selected one who was eager to go into business with Dad. As soon as Dad resigned his job with the oil company, we could no longer live in San Tomé. Mom did not want a small house, and she wanted to take our maid with us. Dad's new partner owned a very large home in Cantaura that was not occupied, and he offered it at a cheap rate.

We Moved to Cantaura

Somehow all of Dad's plans came together. Dad quit the Oil Company, and we moved to Cantaura. Yes, it was the same Cantaura where the chief of police put Dad in jail until Mom got him out. The maid went with us with her youngest baby. She left her other two in the care of her mother, and this Rosa got a week off every month to go home. Our move to Cantaura proved to be an exciting time.

The house had a ten-foot high cinder block fence around the entire property. Broken beer bottles were imbedded in the concrete along the top of the fence to deter thieves. Mom would have really had a fit if she had seen her two sons walking along the top of this wall. We were careful where we stepped and quite lucky Mom never caught is, and lucky because we never fell from the high wall. The wall was designed to discourage thieves, but we demonstrated that in the light of the day it could easily be traversed.

There were more rooms than we could use, but there were

no utilities or indoor plumbing. We had a small gasoline-powered electric generator for light, though it was not powerful enough for anything else. Even an electric iron overloaded it and caused it to shut down. The huge yard inside the fence was paved. Weeds had reclaimed large portions of the pavement on the far side from the house. We rode our bicycles around in it only to discover it was full of nails and broken glass. After using up several inner tube patch kits we had to quit riding our bikes around the paved area. We tried sweeping it but there was more than an acre of pavement, and we wore out Mom's best straw broom trying to clean it up. We swept up a gallon can full of nails and glass shards in one small area near the house. Mom put a stop to our sweeping project when she discovered her broom had no more sweep left in it.

Cantaura was a beautiful, quiet village, and we never saw another roadblock while living there. But we didn't stay in the huge house for long. The problem was that it was too far from Dad's work, and he had to spend several nights a week away. It was also a long way from the commissary, so we kept running short of groceries, and Mom sent Dolores to the local market until we ran out of cash.

Along with the lack of what we today consider more crucial utilities, there was no telephone service in Venezuela when we lived there. This was decades before the invention of cell phones. I remember a presentation in my ninth grade (after we left Venezuela) made by some future thinking person in 1953. The presenter said that in the future people would have their own telephones, that you would be given a telephone number at birth, and it would not change for life, like a Social Security number.

We had not seen Dad for several days when he came home. He definitely had not phoned home to touch base with us. Mom asked him if he had picked up the list of groceries she had given him several days ago. We needed the food, she said, and that she had no dinner for him because there was nothing to eat in the house.

This was not really the truth. We never missed a meal, but Mom was hopping mad. She also had a way of enhancing any story to her advantage. She had not been able to provide the balanced meals she wanted us to have (Spam and bananas fried in lard?) but we never went hungry. That night she was not about to cook him a meal. Dad went out to his truck and brought in a box that contained a five-gallon tin of soda crackers and three one-gallon tins of our favorite Danish brand of powdered milk.

Mom asked where the rest of the groceries were and directed me to go get then in the same breath. His not having them angered her even more. Dad caught hell about that, but we had all the soda crackers and milk we could eat for dinner that night. The crackers and milk were good and filled us up, but mom still threw one hell of a bitch at Dad, one that started that night and lasted until he went back to work. For breakfast we had corn flakes and powdered milk but Mom served Dad some more soda crackers and powdered milk. Dad missed or ignored the point Mom was trying to make. He really liked soda crackers and milk. He left Mom some cash to buy food until he could return with her list of groceries.

Back to El Tigrito

It was no surprise when we moved for the seventh time in Venezuela. This was to a third house in the city of El Tigrito. It was close enough to Dad's work for him to come home every night and not that far from the San Tomé commissary. The house was a larger version of the first house in Venezuela. It faced the very busy road to El Tigre. Neither Mom and Dad particularly liked the house.

I am not sure why Mom never got a car in Venezuela. She never even got a Venezuelan drivers license. It seems that a car would have made life easier for her in Venezuela but it never happened.

We stayed in the seventh house until someone poisoned our pet watchdog and stole our small gasoline powered electric generator. The generator had a long extension cord on it. They picked it up and put the still running generator in the back of a truck and drove it to the end of the extension cord. They turned the generator off, cut the extension cord letting it fall to the ground and drove away. When our lights went out we went out to see if we had run out of gas, only to find the theft. So we moved again, this time with the hope of finding a better and safer neighborhood.

Dad bought the house with glass windows in El Tigrito. It was the same house that was our second house in Venezuela. Dad fixed it up a bit after we moved in. He had the water well cleaned out so it provided us with water, and he hooked an electric pump to the well for filling the water tower in the back yard. He ran water to the kitchen sink, toilet and a shower. No more milk can showers.

Brother and I had to climb into the water tower and clean it out. We climbed into the tank with our bare feet and swept and scraped the dirt out of the bottom and sides, then washed it out with fresh water. The water tower did not have a cover, but Dad did not seem to worry about birds pooping in the water. I mentioned this to Dad and he just told me not to be concerned about it. I thought the addition of bird poop to the tank was sort of like the minnows in the street vendor's water: there was not much we could do about it. Besides, the water seemed to taste good enough when it came out of a faucet in the house. We had flushed out the pipes with fresh well water so the pipes were clean. A few days later some men that worked for Dad came and put a lid on the water tower. It fit like a glove. The wind could not blow it off and birds were out of luck. The installation took less than ten minutes. This must have been why Dad told me not to worry about it.

Theft Prevention

We started collecting dogs for pets and watchdogs. When-ever some Americans that Dad knew left the country we got their pet dog. The plan was not to place the entire burden of protection on a single dog since it would be difficult for a thief to poison all of our dogs.

We stopped taking more dogs after we got to nine dogs. Some of them died, and we got down to six, but we still had enough dogs. The dogs came in all kinds and sizes but mostly they were big and loud—and even the small ones were protec-tive of our house. The Venezuelans really feared dogs but the smart ones seemed to find ways around dogs. Dad was also pretty cagey. He devised a plan to scare the thieves off before they even tried to steal some of our property.

Dad bought a much larger gasoline powered generator. This one was powered with a Chrysler marine engine. You had to start it with a crank. Mom claimed to not have the strength to start it, so that job fell to me. The day it was delivered to our house Dad put his plan into action.

He altered a rattrap by attaching a board full of sharp nails to the metal bar that normally hits the rat, and he gathered all the neighbors and their friends around for a demonstration. After showing them the altered trap with all the sharp nails, he wired the trap to the underside of the generator and armed the trap. When he inserted a piece of wood into the trap as if someone had reached down to pick the generator with the intent of stealing it, the trap made a loud snap, nailing the wood firmly to the trap. Dad demonstrated that he could not pull the wood away and pointed out that a thief could not run away with a hand nailed to the trap. Smiling, Dad told his audience that when someone sprung the trap, he would come out of the house and leisurely dispose of the thief. He picked up a freshly sharpened machete as he asked the neighbors to imagine that the wood nailed to the trap was a thief's arm. He then whacked the wood in half with one sudden hard swing of the machete. Some of the men watching jumped back and gasped as they grabbed their own arms. He chained the generator to the water tower and padlocked the chain. He then wired and soldered the rattrap to the generator. You could see part of the trap but you could not tell it was not armed—nor could it be armed.

It was all still there when we sold the house including the water tower, its cover, the generator and the fake rattrap.

The Last of Felix

Felix started coming to visit us again. We were really pleased about this. He delighted in teaching us things he knew and we did not. He showed us how to use the old crank ice-cream maker someone had given us, one we had never used. All we needed, he said, was rock salt, ice, powdered milk, water and some work turning the crank. Mom even provided some vanilla extract to enhance the flavor. With Felix as a friend, life was good.

One day Felix said he had stayed too long, that he would get home past his deadline. But maybe if he hurried, his mother would not punish him. We loaned him my brother's bike, and he rode away—and he never returned the bike.

Robbed again! we said to each other. This time it was by a person we had called friend. That hurt. Brother Jerry still wants his bike back, though these days you can't find a 1948 boys Schwinn bike with balloon tires.

We did not see Felix for almost a year. When he did show up, the first thing my brother asked him was about the bicycle. His response was that it went away. We told Felix to go away. We never saw him or the bike again. Jerry is still pissed off.

The Candy Man

Rómulo Betancourt was the President when we arrived in Venezuela. His government provided a means for tens of thousands of European World War II refugees and displaced persons to immigrate safely to Venezuela. Each immigrant was allowed 100 kilos of possessions, a total that included including their own body weight. In the case of a mother with a small child it also included the child's weight.

We had the privilege of living a few houses away from one of these couples, the Norayes. She was from Lithuania and he was from Belarus, so technically he was a White Russian, though he disliked being called a Russian. He said that he had been something else, but now he is a Venezuelan. Their daughter was about three when we met them. By then they had been in Venezuela for two years. Each spoke many languages and quickly learned Spanish. He had a Masters degree in Chemistry. He told me he could take any soil sample and determine everything that was in it by exact percentage. One day he showed me one of his most prized possessions: a bamboo slide rule. The lettering on it looked like a combination of Greek and Russian. He said he could calculate anything with it.

The provisions of the immigration did not permit him to use his education, so he had to compete with uneducated Venezuelans for unskilled labor jobs. The law was that native Venezuelans who applied for a job had to be hired first. This rule prevented him from being hired at all because of the high unemployment rate in Caracas at that time, so he searched for something else he could do to make a living. He had worked in a candy factory when he was young, so he asked if he would be allowed to make candy and sell it. The local officials gave him permission on the condition that he moved away from the city of Caracas. By chance he picked El Tigrito.

He made two kinds of hard candy by cooking large sacks of sugar to some exact temperature that he remembered from years before. As it cooled he cut it into chunks, added coloring and flavoring, then put the chunks together into a large roll and stretched it out into long bars about an inch in diameter. The bars either contained orange sections or a flower all through the centers of the bars. The orange sections were orange flavored and the flower candy was mint flavored. He had found these to be the best selling flavors, and made them exclusively.

The Norayes did not have an easy life, but they were happy to be in Venezuela. No other country in the world would take them in. I used to go over and watch them make the candy. After I did many hours of watching, he put me to work. I got pretty good with some of the less arduous tasks. I could cut the long bars into the bite size chucks he sold. When I had been helpful they even paid me with a small amount of candy. I had a real preference for the mint. Once they even paid me in real money for helping them wrap candy. I gave it to Mom and she made them take it back. They still let me help after that, and they always slipped me some of the mint candy even though Mom had directed them not to give me candy. A few pieces of candy always made me happy, need it or not.

The couple became good friends with Mom and Dad. Dad helped him repair his truck from time to time. His wife and Mom often exchanged hardship stories about World War II. The one story I remember took place when she lived under the rule of Hitler.

Trash inspectors examined everyone's trash daily. They read any letters or notes in the trash. If they suspected you were up to no good or had too much food they would arrest you or take away your food. If they found potato peelings in your trash you could be jailed or even executed for wasting food.

Our family had to do without only some things during the

war. Sometimes we missed having particular food items we liked. Doing without was our way of life before and after the Big War. But no one ever threatened us with jail or execution over food or letters.

Our simple house rule on food was that if we had it in the house, it was fair game to be eaten at any time by anyone in the house who was hungry. If a hungry stranger came by and asked, we would always feed them. Often strangers might stay for the night and leave the next day with better clothes than they arrived with. When we were growing I witnessed both Mom and Dad being generous with food and clothing. Sometimes the clothes were items I had outgrown or simply didn't need as bad as did the stranger.

Local Stores

The local food stores were interesting in that we could buy some unusual items in them. They all had a counter, and all the merchandise was behind the counter. If you wanted something the owners put it on the counter and told you the price. If you haggled too much or did not want it they put back. Everything they sold they wrapped in a piece of white butcher paper. If you were lucky a store would have a stalk of finger-length bananas with a distinct apple taste. They called them manzanitas which means little apples.

Commonly sold items were included a scoop of powdered milk, a scoop of sugar, one banana, a chunk of goat milk cheese, one cigarette, twelve and a half cents worth of cassava bread, an empanada dulce, an orange pop, a cold beer. You could even buy a chunk of brown sugar whacked from a large block with a dirty looking machete. Most sales were for one item. They always had iced cold Pepsi and Coke. The high sugar drinks were very popular. They never had root beer, though the stores always had locally bottled, very sweet orange pop.

While we lived in Venezuela they had a 12½ céntimos coin called the locha. Cassava bread is made from a root. Commercially in Venezuela it came in white circular sheets about a meter in diameter and about ½ centimeter thick. It has the consistency of compressed large particle sawdust and all the flavor of cardboard. Cardboard may be easier to chew. Grocers cut it into pie shaped chunks with a sharp Sheetrock knife and a lot of muscle. You could buy about one sixteenth of a circle for a locha. The grocers' goat milk cheese always looked like it had a liberal coating of dirt, but it tasted great, and I never heard of anyone getting sick from eating it. It was a favorite of mine. The empanadas dulce were sweet semi-circular fried pies with a chopped fruit filling. The store owners' wife usually prepared them daily, and they were always delicious.

One day I was in the store across the street from our house with the glass windows. A little girl of about three came in dancing and singing a happy tune. She was dressed in the usual attire for a girl her age. The only thing she had on were gold studs in her pierced ears. The store owner stopped what he was doing and greeted her by name. She smiled cheerfully handed him a note and told him that her mama wanted this. The note was wrapped around some small denomination coins. The storekeeper laid the coins and the note out on the counter and read the note out loud. He then took a single cigarette out of an open package and put it on a fresh piece of white butcher paper. He then went to a small cabinet and opened it. It contained a large pair of scissors and some cigarettes that had been cut in half. He took out half a cigarette and wrapped it in the paper with the whole one. The girl had brought the exact price so he gave her the wrapped package. He thanked the girl for coming in and told her to greet her mama for him. She danced away singing the same happy song. Only after she left did the store owner direct his attention back to the other customers.

Recruiting in El Tigrito

One night we were awakened by people screaming and rifle shots. Soldiers were chasing people all around and shooting at them. Many people yelled and screamed profanities. Dad quickly got us down on the floor against the wall. He leaned our cotton mattress against the wall so that they covered us like a tent. He said this would protect us from stray bullets. After a while everything calmed down. We slept the rest of the night under our mattress.

The next morning there were no dead bodies in the street. Everything looked pretty normal. Dad stayed at home to find out what the revolution was about and who won. He was surprised because none of his workers had told him rumors of an impending revolution. We had to stay in the house until Dad could give us an all clear. Dolores showed up that morning at her usual time. She was her usual cheerful self and acted as if nothing had happened.

Mom quizzed her about the revolution. She just laughed and said there had not been a revolution. It was what they locally called "Hunting Rabbits." She told us that every few years or so the Army would post a notice in the city that they required a certain number of young men to volunteer for the army by some specific date. No one ever volunteered. On some random night as the deadline date approached the army chased down and arrested every man they could catch. The next day if they could prove they were married or not in the draft age range (18-35) they were released. Others were immediately inducted (youngest first) into the army and shipped off for military training. When the quota was reached the army let any remainder go. If they did not reach the quota they simply did another "Rabbit Hunt." We found out that the desertion rate of the Venezuelan Army at that time was one of the lowest in the world. It was just a big game. The recruits resisted with all their might but once caught they really liked being in the military.

Gypsum Business

Another side venture Dad went into was the gypsum business. He found several mountains that were almost pure gypsum. He rented a grader to push several large piles of it up so it could be loaded into dump trucks, and he hired men to manually load the first dump truck load. Gypsum is quite heavy, so the process was extremely labor intensive and slow.

He made little profit on the truck load, but for the enterprise to be profitable it would have to be faster and less dependent on manual labor, so Dad bought a front-end loader. It only took a few scoops using the front-end loader to fill a dump truck.

Secrecy seemed imperative. If the cement plant where he sold the gypsum discovered the location of the gypsum, he was sure they would bypass him and extract the gypsum themselves. So when the dump truck was full the driver went to an area away from the gypsum source where he washed the truck. A day or so later he drove the gypsum to a cement factory. Dad never disclosed the location of the gypsum to the people running the cement factory.

It was located between the city of Cantaura and the cement plant. Surely they have discovered that by now. The oil companies had mapped hundreds of large deposits of gypsum and other valuable minerals besides oil. The chief executive officers of the North American oil companies had no interest in other natural resources besides the oil they were harvesting. They had the geologists map everything of future value and file the maps away for future reference. All these documents surely belong to the Venezuelan government now. The country is full of untapped natural resources.

Dad's mining and selling gypsum did not make much money and took a lot of time. Initially Dad thought he would be able to just scoop the gypsum up like dirt with the front-end loader, but the rock was too hard for the loader. Some of the sheets of the clear gypsum were about a foot thick, six feet wide and many yards long. Gypsum is not a hard rock, but the small front-end loader was not powerful enough to scoop up large chunks of gypsum. It took a tractor to break it up into a loadable form, and to mine gypsum on a large scale it had to be blown up before a tractor could do much. Dad decided not to devote any more of his life in this venture, so he got out of the business.

He found a buyer for the front-end loader and sold it. The buyer came to our house with 20,000 Bolivares in cash, carrying it in a large brown paper grocery sack. The money was in 10, 20, 50 and 100 Bolivar notes with most of it in 20 Bolivar notes. It made quite a pile when they dumped it out on the kitchen floor for counting. The kitchen had no windows facing the street, and the floor seemed safer to the adults than the table. All the adults pitched in to sort the bills by size and then make even-valued stacks of cash. We kids watched out of curiosity for a while but it made the buyer nervous so Mom asked us to go in the other room. She also told us we could not go outside or have anyone over while the money was in the house. The money was counted five or six times before everyone was confident that it was correct. Dad then put the money back into the brown paper sack. He covered the top of the sack with some old newspaper to disguise its contents.

There were no banks in El Tigrito. The closest one was in Barcelona. So Dad took the sack of cash to a local priest, who had the only safe in town that Dad knew about. He felt comfortable using this safe. Dad wrote his name on the sack in pencil and left it on a shelf in an empty spot of the priest's large unlocked safe. The safe sat in the house where the priest lived. He told Dad that he never locked the safe and that nothing had ever been stolen from it. Most people did not know the safe existed, and the ones that did, the priest said, would fear stealing from the church. If Dad ever needed the money when the priest happened to be away from the house, he could tell one of the nuns, then retrieve his money.

All of the money was all still in the paper sack several days later when Dad picked it up. He had used the priest's safe many times before as a bank. The priest had cashed large oil company checks for Dad, allowing him to pay his employees in a timely manner. The priest had a courier that made trips to the bank in Barcelona as needed.

The Healer

One day Dad was supervising his Cracker Jack team of workers as they took apart a steel pipeline to move it to another location. The pipeline went down into a small canyon. Dad decided he should disconnect the joints going over the edge so none of his workers would get hurt. He unbolted the flange connecting the pipe that went into the canyon. Once free the pile swung around toward him instead of away from him as he had guessed. The pipe caught him by the left knee and pinned him to the ground. His workers laughed and poked fun at Dad for trying to do their work as they lifted the four inch steel pipe from his leg.

Nothing appeared to be broken, but his knee hurt like the devil and became swollen. He had to hobble around on crutches to see the American doctor, who took X-rays and told him no bones were broken, though he had some damage to tissue and ligaments, which would take a long time to heal. There was nothing else the doctor could do for it.

After a few weeks one of Dad's workers asked Dad why he had not gone to the local healer. He explained to Dad that the healer was empowered by God and could not accept anything for helping or he would lose his healing power. After several more days of pain and agony Dad was ready for anything. Mom and Dad went with the worker to the healer's home. They were instructed to bring a large white towel and a bottle of rum. They were told that when they left they must take the towel and unused rum with them.

The healer had Dad lie on a cot and placed the towel under his injured knee. He then washed Dad's leg and knee with some of the rum, using the towel to prop up the leg and catch the excess rum. The healer said some prayers and appeared to go into a trance. He moved a crucifix over Dad's leg and touched the injured area in a crisscross pattern moving up the leg. As the crucifix got close to the leg the tissue moved up to meet the crucifix, and when they touched the pain subsided. The healer continued moving the crucifix up the leg with the same results. As Dad watched he thought what he saw was impossible, that it could not be happening. At that instant it stopped working.

The healer looked at Dad and told him that he had lost his faith. He told Dad he could not help anyone without faith, and that he must leave immediately and not come back without faith. Mom and Dad took the towel and the rest of the rum with them. The healer warned them again not to leave any gift or he would lose his power to heal. Dad walked out without the crutches. The part of the leg that had touched the crucifix appeared to be well. The rest of the leg got better over time. Dad never went back to the healer.

Gold and Diamond Hunting

The contracting business went into a slump. Abruptly there was no work. It was rumored that the oil company wanted to demonstrate their power over the wage demands of the common workers. This was a good story and it had a ring of truth to it, but the cause did not really matter: Dad was out of work.

The situation made it the perfect time for Dad to go try his luck mining diamonds and gold along the Orinoco and Caroní rivers. He hired a guide. They loaded a jeep and trailer with provisions and went away for several months. Dad left Mom with some cash and arranged for us to charge groceries at the store down the street. The local stores operated on such a small margin that by us owing them about the equivalent of over one hundred dollars for several months likely helped put the store out of business.

When Dad came back he had a small yellow diamond and a small piece of gold he had found. The gold was smaller than the head of a kitchen match, and the diamond was about half the size of the gold. The diamond was in the shape of a slightly flattened dodecahedron, and it had some flaws in it. The shape supposedly gave the diamond secret mystical powers. If it really did we never recognized any of them. Dad was excited and had lots of stories to tell about the people he had met.

One was a Spaniard who was a geologist. He explained to Dad that his test to see if a stone was a diamond was wrong. Dad assumed that diamonds were so hard that they would not break when hit with a hammer. Dad said that he had probably destroyed hundreds of diamonds before the Spaniard stopped him. The one small diamond was the only one he ever brought back. It was too small and flawed for jewelry but was a beautiful thing to study.

Dad neglected to tell Mom that he had hired a young woman to cook for him. Later I found out she did a lot more than cook.

The Spaniard had found a rich vein of gold, one he could not mine consistently without drawing attention to a specific area. If the landowner suspected a rich vein had been discovered he would advertise it in all the communities near the find, which would result in hundreds of locals swarming in and covering the area with small pit mines. This would allow the landowner to provide them food in exchange for the gold they mined each day. When the rich vein was mined out, the crowd would leave, and the landowner would have all the gold they had mined. All the small pit mines would be left as a reminder of the hard work and good times.

The goal of the Spaniard was to accumulate 100,000 US dollars in gold and leave. Dad got word before we left Venezuela that he had accomplished his mission and was leaving the country. That same amount of gold today would be worth around three million US dollars.

The Lykes Lines

Mom threw such a bitch about Dad's absence that he got a haircut and left our house the next day. He was gone this time for over a month. When he came back he and Mom decided that it was time to leave Venezuela, that they take a freighter that booked a limited number of passengers. The freighters usually followed the coast and made stops in some of the coastal islands on the way to the States, a trip that sounded like it would be a lot of fun. It was also cheaper than airfare home.

Dad sold the house. Instead of a yard sale we gave the candy man and his wife most of the possessions we could not take with us. Dad sold the jeep but not the pickup. The candy man drove us to Puerto La Cruz in the pickup, and there Dad gave it to him. This was when we left the last Rosa (Dolores) for good. We never saw her again but Mom missed her for the rest of her life. If it had been possible she would have brought the woman and her three children back with us and kept her as a maid forever. The trip to the coast was our eighth move in Venezuela but not our last.

We moved into this cheap hotel until we could catch a Lykes Line freighter home. We were looking forward to a month long cruise and seeing all the countries along the way from Venezuela to Texas. Unfortunately, we had just missed one freighter, and the next available one was three weeks off— but we never boarded a Lykes Line Freighter.

The first night in that cheap hotel was noisy. The second night it sounded like people were running across the roof chasing and screaming at one another, and the next day there were a lot of police around. When Dad asked what was going on, he discovered that the motel was in the middle of a red light district, and all the noise came from the police were chasing prostitutes and pimps. Some of them ran across the roof and the police went after them. The police explained that our rooms were normally rented by the hour and recommended we find better accommodations. They even suggested a good neighborhood.

Life in a Hotel on the Beach

We had no pickup, so Dad walked around until he found a hotel in the recommended area. He rented two rooms, and we moved to them in a taxi that day. They were in an old hotel across the street from the beach.

The walls of the rooms were made of boards not nailed real tightly together and had been covered with wall paper many years before we got there. The poor construction meant we had to be quiet in the rooms to avoid disturbing other guests, though after a few days we discovered the hotel had few guests. It was not a high class place. A few guests came for a day or two and then left. Unlike people in the motel in the red light district, our new neighbors were quite nice, and I quickly learned to like the hotel. A few strides from the front door and we could swim in the beautiful Caribbean Sea.

Sometimes we would walk around to a rocky area to the right of the hotel and catch some small fish that lived around the rocks. Most of these fish were not much more than three inches long, but they were fun to catch.

The fish hooks sold in Venezuela were very strange. The shank ends did not have the expected eye for connecting the leader or line. They only contained a flattened end on the shank. We had to learn to tie around the shank a special knot that looked like a hangman's noose. Until we learned to make the knot tight around the shank we lost a lot of hooks. Clip on leaders and swivels were not available while we were in

Venezuela.

The Carribean at the edge of Puerto La Cruz has almost no tide. Tall islands form a semicircle around the beaches, and these islands keep the waves to a minimum. Many mornings the water was as smooth as glass so the blue of the sky and sea blended creating the illusion that the islands were floating in the sky.

One morning Dad went for a walk down the beach looking for fresh flounder. He found that flounder was not a popular fish. The natives did not like them because both eyes were on the same side of the head, a condition that spooked them. Instead of flounder he came back with a job at a Nelson Rockefeller experimental fisheries foundation called Pesquerias Caribes. At the fishery Dad met an American from Maine who was running the business. When Dad told him that he could build the apparatus needed to trawl for shrimp he hired Dad. The idea behind the enterprise was to interest the locals enough that they would copy the modern fishing processes. Dad worked at this job for the next eighteen months.

Dad got his shrimping experience when I was in the third grade and our family lived on Mustang Island. This is a small island at the end of Padre Island on the coast of Texas. Dad's middle brother had a shrimp boat. When the weather was too bad to work construction they would go shrimping. Sometimes like little boys with a toy—in this case a shrimp boat—they could not resist playing with, Dad and his brother went shrimping regardless of the weather. Their trips were never moneymakers. I remember the day they brought home a five-gallon bucket of bay shrimp, their total catch for a three-day trip. They divided the shrimp and that's what we had to eat until it was gone. Shrimp beat the hell out of soda crackers and powdered milk. We kids got to head and peel the shrimp, then Mom boiled some and fried the rest.

We made several friends in and around the hotel. Among them was a family of Spaniards who ran a grocery store less than a block away, a place where we shopped. They had a daughter about Sue's age. Sue and the girl became very good friends. When the Spanish girl took typing and shorthand in Spanish at a local college, Sue took the courses with her.

La Cucaracha

Dad got tired of walking to work so he bought a small car, an old English Ford. I do not recall what year it was made. It could have been anywhere from a 1935 to a 1948 model. The English Ford from those years all looked similar, and like all truly old Fords it was painted black. It was so tiny that we barely all fit into it. I remember the nice upholstery in the back seat, which was wonderful compared to anything we ever had in the back of a pickup. The locals called our little black car La Cucaracha. It looked even smaller when Dad put his five foot ten 240-pound body in it. Everyone in our neighborhood knew the Cucaracha driven by the big fat American, and everywhere Dad drove it, people laughed. We enjoyed it for about a year.

An Affair

The hotel managers were a young Italian couple. The first thing we noticed about them was that they did not want anyone to see the inside of their room. They would open the door only wide enough to get in or out and then close it fast. It then became a challenge for us kids to stand around and try to get a glimpse of the room's contents, but it never worked. We never saw the inside of their room.

We did notice that a very large man came around often. He was bigger than Dad and always had a large hunting knife strapped to his right hip. When he arrived the husband left and the man with the knife took the manager's wife into the secret room for about an hour. We could hear them laughing and having a good time in the room. Sometimes the wife came out wearing a different dress. This activity made the manager angry, but his wife seemed to enjoy it. The manager never did anything about it. It looked to me like this knife-carrying bastard was coming over two or three times a week and screwing the manager's wife, but what the hell did I know? I was only twelve. I will never know what the husband got out of the deal, and even if I knew, I doubt that I would understand why he let it continue.

Just another Revolution

Our hotel turned out to be in close proximity of the next revolution, for the local Police Station was just a block away. Friends and co-workers of Dad's kept telling him that on a certain day he and his family must stay inside to avoid harm or being shot, that it would not be safe for anyone to be on the street that day. It was no coincidence that three days before this special date we moved about a mile down the beach into a Quonset house owned by Pesquerias Caribes.

The day before this not so secret revolution the police rounded up and jailed most of the dissidents all over the country. There was no fanfare or publicity. The army simply went around and made arrests in most major cities in Venezuela, but they missed the group in Puerto La Cruz, an oversight that got the local dissidents killed.

Dad, my brother and I were on the pier at Pesquerias Caribes on that special day when the shooting started. We moved out closer to the end of the pier for a better view and watched with interest as soldiers ran down to the beach in front of the hotel where we had been living. They lifted their automatic rifles above their heads and over a sand embankment to fire random bursts at anything that moved, doing no aiming. Mostly they fired down the street in the general direction of the police station. Bullets struck our old hotel, the Spaniards' store and several other buildings in the neighborhood.

Mom came out to the pier and yelled at Dad to get back, but he ignored her. She asked Dad how far the rifle bullets could go and still kill someone. He said about five miles, and he seemed to suddenly realize how close we were. We hurried back from the pier to a safer area. Dad wanted to sneak back to the pier but Mom managed to keep him away until the shooting was over. The entire revolution thing took less than half an hour.

The next day the local paper reported that twelve men rushed into the police station armed with one old rusty pistol and eleven machetes. The police, in spite of being armed with automatic rifles, ran out the back of the police station and down to the beach before they fired a single shot. The paper reported the names of twelve revolutionaries that the police managed to kill. The thirteenth coffin we counted in the funeral procession was not accounted for in the news report. Perhaps it was an unlucky bystander. We never found out for sure. The paper went on to explain that arrests were made the previous day of many dissidents to prevent such actions from happening all over the country. The army took credit for having squelched a national revolution, and life went on as usual except for those in jail or dead.

The next revolution took place in November, 1950. The sitting Venezuelan president was assassinated, an event that we read about in the local newspaper.

The papers at the time said that his assassin wanted to be the president, but he lacked control of the military. The assassin was quickly identified and shot to death while resisting arrest. The local newspaper said the arrest was peaceful enough until the arresting police started harassing the suspect. After some shoving, pushing and hitting, the assassin took a swing at the police, and that's when the police shot him to death. The newspaper also reported a rumor that the assassin was killed because there was no death penalty in Venezuela.

The death of the president resulted in a fast change of control in a rich country. The group in charge of the military appointed an interim president, a man who stayed in office for about two years. He stepped aside, and the military installed another of their own as president. All the political changes at high levels had no impact on our lives. Everything in our world continued without change.

Local Catches

Dad's work at the fisheries proved fun and interesting. My brother and I went out on the shrimp boat with Dad many times. The small shrimp net pulled in some really big shrimp. In the lingo of shrimp size, it takes 16 of size 16 shrimp (considered jumbos) to make a pound. We watched Dad's net dump out some size one shrimp: it took one of them to make a pound.

My brother and I went swimming almost every day. It was less than one hundred yards from our house to the edge of the water. We often walked to the end of the company pier and jumped into the water, and we would swim for hours.

Sometimes we swam to a large boat that was anchored about a hundred yards beyond the end of the pier, a boat owned by the fisheries foundation though it had not been used for years. The anchor chain and bottom of the craft were encrusted with oysters. Small fish and baby octopuses swam in abundance around the anchor chain. Sometimes we climbed aboard the boat to dive off for fun. Dad's boss saw us on the boat one day and we were told not to board her anymore. But we still swam out there with a bucket and a knife to scrape oysters for Mom. She loved them raw.

One day we saw a boy in a rowboat diving for something, so we swam out to see what he was doing. He was diving to the bottom and picking up living conch shells that were three to four inches long and putting them in the boat. There were hundreds of them all over the bottom. He told us that his family and neighbors were going to boil and eat them that night, so we helped him catch all he wanted. He threw back the smaller ones and asked us to catch only the bigger ones. We were invited to the feast that night but we missed it.

The conchs must have migrated in from deeper water and moved because a few days later there were none to be found.

Some Saturdays we went to a theater where the shows were American movies with Spanish subtitles, and the theater showed the same serials we might see in the American theaters. The difference was that the Venezuelans would not put up with waiting for ten or twelve Saturdays to see a serial. If a serial dragged on for too many weeks, the audience would trash the theater and leave, so the theater managers showed the entire serial production in two or three Saturdays.

It was on a movie Saturday that a whale shark showed up in the Puerto La Cruz bay. The beast attracted a lot of attention. The natives spotted it when it was several miles away, and a crowd came out to the pier to see it. It swam between the end of the pier and the boat we played on. Dad saw the shark and nearly went into hysterics looking for his sons. Fortunately everyone seemed to know that the whale shark is a plankton-feeder and would not know what to do with two young boys. All the swimmers got out of the water anyway. Sadly we were at the movies and missed the shark, but we heard plenty about it. The creature was forty to sixty feet long, depending on the person telling us about it. Mom made it bigger than Dad, so it was probably around forty feet long.

I still regret seeing the last five parts of a Zorro serial instead of the whale shark. Our native friends all said the serial was too long and should have ended the week before, and this time I agreed with them. Dad got to see another whale shark when he was out on a trip without us, so we completely missed seeing a whale shark. Darn!

The coastal waters were teeming with life, and we did see a sperm whale playfully tossing her baby up in the air. The mother would come up under the baby and toss it sixty or seventy feet up in the air. The baby looked larger than our English Ford. Dad's boat captain, a man who had been a harpooner on a whaler out of Trinidad when he was a teenager, wanted to take the shrimp boat closer so he could get a better look. Dad did not want the mother to mistake his boat for a baby whale or an enemy, so we kept our distance.

Once we saw a school of porpoise, a gigantic school about fifty yards wide and about a mile long. They swam fast and appeared to have a destination in mind. We were going in the opposite direction but we slowed down to watch them pass. Another time we took an overnight trip along the coast toward Cumana to pick up a load of Spanish mackerel for the company. At night the water was full of phosphorescence, so anything that moved in the water made it sparkle and glow. We saw a school of sardines that seemed to fill the sea between two islands that were more than a mile apart.

One overnight trip we anchored behind some long sand islands. The deck hand baited several large hooks fastened to heavy-duty lines about a quarter inch in diameter. He tied these lines firmly to the boat. He then chummed up the water with some of the trash fish we netted during the day, fish that had been ripening in the sun. His goal was to catch shark that he planned to salt and dry, then sell the meat for extra money when we returned. He caught a few small ones about three feet long and was excited about catching more. This is when each baited line was stretched to its limit and snapped in rapid succession. The Captain said that the big boys had arrived, and the shark fishing was over for the night. He cautioned us not to fall overboard. Dad made us sleep in the boat's small cabin that night.

A Goat Hunting Party

The locals did not like what Dad was doing with the shrimp boat. Instead of being impressed with the large shrimp being caught and wanting to emulate the process, they tried to get Dad arrested to stop him. The only shrimp they wanted to catch were small shrimp in shallow pools along the coast. They would work all day with a cast net to catch a few kilos of shrimp. The really big ones would be less than three decimeters. Dad tried to get to know some of the local businessmen so he could understand what they had against his way of catching shrimp, and he had hopes of finding a way of changing this attitude.

Dad took our family and a group of the businessmen on a party one Saturday. We went to an island about nine miles away called El Borracho. Only wild goats inhabited it. The goats were supposed to have been left there by the Spanish pirates so they would have some food when they returned, but the pirates quit returning and the goats stayed and thrived. They ate cactus and other hardy island plants. There was no fresh water on the island except for the occasional rain. It was reported that the goats sometimes drank seawater. Whatever they did, the hardy goats prospered for generations.

Everyone brought food and drink with them to this party. One man even brought rifles to shoot the wild goat, though it was illegal to own a rifle of any kind in Venezuela. You could own shotguns or muzzle loaders, but not rifles. So the guns were well disguised as they were transported to and from the boat. The man that owned the rifles picked out the gun he wanted and offered the others to anyone who wanted to kill a goat.

A group of men including Dad took the rifles and ventured beyond our temporary camp to shoot a goat or two. The Island was a steep mountain jutting out of the Caribbean Sea. The steep rocky cliffs were covered with cactus and other unfriendly plants. There were some goat trails leading down to the small beach where we anchored the boat. We could even see some goats way up near the top of the mountain. These "stupid" goats had been hunted before, so when the rifles came out, they ran to the other side of the island and were not seen for the rest of the day. The hunters returned hours later, all sweaty and cursing the stupid goats for not making easy targets. The only thing any of them got was stuck several times by cactus. There was no goat to roast. They all swore to get one the next time and drank a lot of beer to confirm the oath. Dad said the party was a success but his boss told him not to do another one. It seemed that Dad should have invited his boss to the party.

Today the island is part of the very large Venezuelan National Park of Mochima, which covers 949.35 square kilometers. We had the pleasure of playing there before it was a National park.

Shrimping and the Law

The reason the locals were against trawling was simple. They thought it was killing off the future game fish they depended on for a living. Dad's crew threw overboard the trash fish caught by trawling, and some of the dead fish washed up on the beaches. This scared the local fishermen who concluded that trawling would kill most of the fish, putting an end to the way they made a living.

There is an abundance of life in the sea around Puerto La Cruz. The shrimping may have done some harm over time.

The police came to arrest Dad for trawling for shrimp. After a lengthy discussion with Dad and his boss, they decided not to arrest Dad this time, but if he went trawling for shrimp again they promised to arrest his boss. After that, Dad abandoned the use of the trawl net and started taking the boat out to catch deep-sea fish, and he let his boss fight the political battle.

There was an area where the water was over 100 fathoms deep. The natives hauled out large red snapper and grouper from this trench. Some of the grouper weighed several hundred pounds. Dad and crew went to the trench many times and never caught a single thing.

We met Nelson Rockefeller when he came to visit Pesquerias Caribes. After that he went to Caracas to get permission to continue with the trawling and other activities, but the government official who could grant the permits was never available to meet with him.

Nearly sixty years later Venezuela amended their fishing laws, which included an attempt to allow trawl fishing. The local fishermen lobbied against elements of the proposed law with the same argument they worked sixty years ago against Dad and the Pesquerias Caribes. They claimed trawling would kill off the fish that they caught for a living. The local fishermen proved still to be a powerful group. Since March 2008 it is still illegal to do any kind of trawl fishing in all Venezuelan waters.

The Real Reason We Went Home

Dad's role in Pesquerias Caribes seemed to be disappearing. Then one day a friend of Dad's came over, one of the people at the party who owned a chain of stores. He was the one that furnished the rifles for the goat hunt. The newspapers had linked him with some criminal activity, but to me he always seemed really nice. He had visited several times before and had always been friendly and polite. This time he had not come to visit with Dad.

He brought my older sister a dozen red roses. While we were not looking Sue had transformed into a beautiful young woman. The man asked Dad for permission to court his oldest daughter. Dad told him that he was very honored by this offer—but the reality was that Dad knew the man had a wife and several mistresses. In less than a month we were all in Texas.

This time Dad was in no mood to wait for a freighter. We

went home by plane with stops in Bogotá, Colombia and Panama City, Panama. In Colombia Dad had to bribe an official to allow us back on the plane, something Dad and Mom had anticipated. Dad took out his wallet removed all the cash in it, then asked the official if he would take all the money he had in the world to support his family. The man basically said yes as he grabbed the cash from Dad's hand and shoved it in his own pocket. We were then allowed back on the plane, so we scurried aboard and waited eagerly for the plane to take off. Mom had the main stash of our money hidden away before we took off for Colombia.

Panama was great in 1952, even if it was hot and humid during our stay. We visited three days without incident, and we found everyone to be friendly. We even went across the Panama Canal on bridges several times. To us everything seemed a lot cleaner and more modern than in Venezuela.

My Dad was arrested twice in a foreign country. Both times Mom bribed some official and got him out of jail. We moved eight times in the four and a half years we lived in Venezuela. We lived in a total of eight places if you include the two nights we spent in a red light district motel, and we lived twice in the house with glass windows. That's what happened in our family. What did your family do for excitement when you were growing up?

We moved another six times before I finished high school. Sue was right. We really were itinerant, no doubt about it.

Postscript

Dad finally moved us into an old house Stadium Road in Port Arthur, Texas. He lived there for ten or eleven years with Mom and Gail after the rest of us grew up and moved on. The arrangement for the house was a six percent loan on six thousand dollars for the house, to be paid to a homebuilder friend of Dad's. Dad never paid a cent on the principal. He paid only the six percent interest and the taxes on the house.

This house had several spirits in it, and one of them really did not like Susan's husband David King. One Saturday afternoon it threw him bodily out of Gail's bed when he was trying to take a quiet nap. He and Mom could not find a priest who would do an exorcism, but they did find a priest that blessed the house. The old Priest sprinkled holy water and prayed in every room, hall and closet he could walk into. The spirit that tossed David out of Gail's bed must have left, but the one in Gail's closet stayed. I would rarely go into her room and would definitely not peek into her closet. Walking up the stairs and heading towards her room always made the hair on the back of my neck stand up even long before the blessing. I would never walk up the stairs at night without turning on the light.

The spirit in the laundry room never left either. It turned on the clothes dryer at odd times. Dad was sure there was a loose wire in the dryer hookup, so he redid the wiring and even replaced the switches in the dryer, but the dryer still turned itself on. Sometimes it happened in the middle of the night when no one was around. The running dryer would wake Mom. She would go turn it off and fuss loudly at whatever was turning the dryer on. One night I even saw her out of frustration bang on the dryer with a broom. Mom even put a heavy book on the door of the dryer to keep open as the dryer could not run with the door open, but the book kept being shoved off the door with a bang, the door would close and the dryer would turn on.

The city renamed Stadium Road, and later the house burned down. I hope the spirits found a better place to stay. The old house provided a treasure of memories. You probably would not believe most of them either, but we lived through the good and the bad of them.

You Can't Bully Everyone

First Grade Bully

GA was oldest of three sons of a Baptist minister who worked as a carpenter because he was self-ordained, a man with no formal education who could not get assigned to a church that had enough money to support his family. While GA was growing up his family moved around a lot as his father sought work.

Every time they moved, GA had to work his way through a new grade school pecking order, which usually meant going through an assessment process until someone in the current pecking order decided he could beat up GA. At that point GA had to fight, and if he won, the process had to be repeated until he lost or no one else wanted to fight.

One school already had resident a bully that was bigger and stronger than everyone else. He was a redhead who was repeating the first grade for the second or third time. The first day of school he announced his superiority and beat GA up. The second day of school he beat GA up again and pushed him into a muddy ditch, for the redhead liked winning the scraps. He made every day more of the same. GA got beat up and muddy on the way to school and again on the way home. GA dreaded going to school because he knew the bully would knock GA down and get his clothes all muddy, a situation that caused even more problems for GA. His mother had to hand wash his clothes and really fussed at him for getting muddy every day.

Finally GA had enough. When the bully came over to knock him down the muddy ditch anger surged through GA's entire body. He lowered his head and ran at the bully full steam, butted him in the gut and knocked the breath out of him. Before the bully could get up GA jumped on the boy's chest. He then sat down hard on his soft stomach. Before the kid recovered from that, GA grabbed the red hair with both fists and started pounding his head in the dirt and rocks. They skirmished and rolled into the ditch with GA still on top. GA screamed in the redhead's ears that he was going to kill the bully. He then pushed the bully's head under the water in the ditch while continuing to scream that he was going to kill him.

He probably would have done just that but for a good adult Christian woman that heard the fracas. She jumped in and pulled the first graders out of the ditch and held them apart. The woman recognized GA as the minister's son. She tried to shame GA with that bit of information, then walked him home where the minister beat GA with a leather belt. No amount of beating would make him say he was sorry. He would just say that the next time he had to fight the bully he would kill him, and after a while the minister stopped the beating.

Life gradually got back to semi-normal, though there were a few changes. First the bully no longer wanted to fight or have anything to do with GA, choosing instead to take his scratched and bruised face away from GA as fast as he could. Secondly, the trip to and from school became quite pleasant. The best part of all for GA was that his mother was off his back because he no longer came home with muddy clothes. A few months later the minister and his family moved again. The next town had another grade school with another pecking order to establish. Life was tough in 1920.

The Third Grade Bully

Another time and another school, GA found himself in the third grade. This school had its own self-appointed school bully, one who did not limit bullying to the third grade students. He bullied everyone in school—which included all six grades. He didn't single out GA for any kind of special treatment.

This bully had learned to keep his sheep in line with a long switch. Every day he cut a fresh flexible limb about four feet long from a mesquite tree. He trimmed off all the foliage to make made a functional whip for popping everyone he could catch. He cackled with joy when his victim yelped in pain. GA did not know the drill so he got popped the first day on the arm. It stung like the dickens and raised a big welt. Other kids told GA to expect such treatment daily and to learn to stay out of the way. No teachers were ever around to stop the bully. All the tormented students were afraid of retribution if they reported the problem.

The next day GA was ready for him. He too had a pocket knife, one he used to cut a fresh limb about five feet long from an acacia tree. He trimmed up a nice handle and removed all the three-inch thorns except for a clump of them on the business end of the weapon. The switch must have looked like a small Stegosaur's tail. When he swung it through the air it made a loud swish, causing everyone near to run away, though GA's only target was the bully. GA popped him in the butt with the thorns.

To everyone's surprise and specially GA's the thorns pierced the boy's pants and stuck. It was like they had been nailed in so GA could not pull them out. GA tried yanking hard on the neatly trimmed handle, but the thorns seemed to dig in deeper. GA was afraid to turn the handle loose so he continued to pull on the handle.

The more GA yanked, the louder the boy screamed. The thorns were solidly in the bully's butt. When GA pulled the bully had no choice but to scream louder and back up. The fun finally came to an end when some adults showed up to see what was causing all the screaming. They took the boys into the office with an adult carefully holding the switch to keep it from pulling on the kid's butt. The thorns had to be individually cut off the switch with wire cutters, then yanked out one at a time with a pair of pliers. Only then could the pants be removed to expose the wounds. The appointed school nurse then slathered copious amounts of iodine over the area. This must have burned and stung because the kid screamed and cried even more.

There was hell to pay for that trick. It was just the second day in a new school and GA was causing trouble again, so he got another thrashing with his Dad's leather belt. Corporal punishment was the order of the day, but it never made GA repent. The teachers all were all furious because the incident got them assigned to guard duty over the little beasts in the mornings before school. No more resting quietly until school started when they had to let the beasts in. They wanted to expel GA, but they only had to wait a few weeks for the minister and family to move to another town and another school with another pecking order to establish.

Some Boys Just have to be Bad

GA grew up with two uncles. One was a little younger than GA's Dad and the other uncle was one day younger than GA. The older uncle often took the younger boys fishing and worked to teach them the ways of the world. This uncle smoked, chewed, drank, cursed and chased women. He also did countless other vile things the preacher would rather not have the boys know about. According to the minister he was true hedonist and therefore full of the devil. He was against anything the Baptist Church stood for and expressed his lack of faith to anyone that would listen to him, including his preacher brother. These traits made the younger boys love him.

One Sunday he took the boys fishing in his favorite catfish hole in the river. The fishing ended when the GA's Dad appeared with a crowd of sinners, some there to be baptized and the others as witnesses to the saving of their friends and neighbors. The fishermen brother looked on in disgust as the preacher and sinners waded into the water waist deep, an event that ended fishing for the day. Just as the first woman was about to be immersed she burst out with a loud emotional "Thank the Lord I've been saved." The reprobate fisherman and uncle knew her well, and he responded with an even louder "And not a god damn bit too soon either, sister." He then he spit a big chaw of tobacco into the river. She appeared to be so angry when she was immersed in the water to wash her sins away that GA, telling the story years later, always wondered if that baptism really took.

GA tried to emulate his older uncle's tobacco habit and was caught by his Dad with a plug of tobacco in his mouth. To GA's surprise his Dad did not beat him this time. Instead he took GA to the store and spent some hard earned coin on a popular brand of chaw. It surprised GA that his Dad knew the brand by name—the same brand his uncle used. GA was initially pleased. Then he told GA that if he was old enough to chew he should chew like a man. He had GA take an extra big mouthful and chew on it. When GA was ready to spit his Dad told him that real men did not spit. He told him to swallow the whole slug. He made him take in another big chaw. After repeating this a few times GA started vomiting so intensely that he thought he was about to die, for he had never been so sick in his life. He never chewed or smoked again. Just the smell of tobacco made him ill the rest of his life.

Hunter Gatherer

In 1928 GA lived in the Rio Grande area near Presidio, Texas. His Dad picked the area from a map of the United States while the family lived in Oklahoma. He figured they would have to grow a lot of their own food to survive the depression, and the Rio Grande area of Texas looked as if it would support a garden year round.

GA turned fourteen that year. His birthday present was a .22 caliber long rifle pistol and a case of one thousand cartridges. This was not a toy for play or target practice. It was serious business. GA, a crack shot and a good hunter was expected to use the pistol for bringing home enough game on a regular basis to help feed the family. Until the gift of the pistol, he hunted with a borrowed shotgun. But there were problems with such hunting. For one thing, shells were expensive, and the shotgun was not always available. Another problem was with concealing the shotgun, something GA had to do because the only hunting land available was on private posted property. If caught he would be arrested and the gun was subject to confiscation.

Sometimes GA and his family lived in a rental house, but most of the time their residence was a tent. GA's mother made her three sons take turns with the cooking and cleaning chores. GA hated to cook. He would bargain with his brothers in trying to trade his turn cooking for other chores. He even tried to make the food taste bad to encourage chore swaps. Once he added soap to the beans to encourage his brothers to trade with him, a trick that earned him some severe punishment.

The family stove was usually an outside wood fire pit with steel spikes in the ground to hold the pot, a large cast iron Dutch oven used for cooking most meals. Sometimes the family used the Dutch oven for homemade cornbread, and sometimes it served to cook pinto beans. The family found rabbit, dove or other small game a welcome addition to any meal, especially since meat was not an item they could afford. Procuring meat became GA's responsibility when he was fourteen and got the gift of the pistol.

GA often walked out of town, then sneaked through the barbed wire fence onto a large posted cattle ranch, working to dodge the fence riders who rode horseback around the ranch. They rigorously monitored the ranch, and all were armed with saddle rifles. They did not want anyone hunting around the owner's cattle, and they especially did not want to lose any cattle to poachers or rustlers. GA usually went out at dusk after the fence riders had made their last round for the day.

He had a canvas bag that would hold a few rabbits or quail and carried it folded and tucked under his shirt. This kept it from being so obvious that he was going hunting. It was not unusual for GA to be out all night hunting. Sometimes after bagging some rabbits, he came across a group of Mexicans walking across the border in search of a better life. GA knew that, bad as it was in the USA during the Depression, it was worse in Mexico. His habit was to greet the people in fluent Spanish, and he often offered to share his rabbits with them if they would do the cooking. Seldom did the people he met refuse his offer. After eating mesquite roasted rabbit they would usually sleep on the ground for a while, then leave well before sunup. Everyone seemed to know when the fence riders would show up and did their best to avoid them. In the early morning hours GA had time to shoot more rabbits before going home.

One day GA came across a group of peccaries foraging in the underbrush. The common name for these pig look-alikes is javelina. GA often saw javelinas, but it was the first time such a large group of them had wandered this close to him. These docile-appearing animals are not afraid of anyone or anything. They have strong sharp tusks that can cause serious wounds. They ignored GA and went about their business of foraging, but he decided to add one to the food pot. He looked them over and decided a small one would be best since he would have to carry it over ten miles in his canvas bag to get it home. So he picked out the smallest one and shot it. It squealed and fell over dead.

About a dozen of the large tuskers chased GA up a tree. They repeatedly slashed at the tree with their tusks while squealing and grunting to let GA know how angry they were at him. GA was unaware that peccaries form social groups and fiercely defend each other. They kept GA in the tree for a long time before seeming to leave. Every time he climbed out of the tree and approached the dead peccary, they rushed back at him with a vengeance. They finally moved away in one direction. When he could not hear their grunting GA rushed off in the opposite direction. The one he shot did not make it to the pot, and he never shot another one.

Several times while he was hunting he heard the fence riders approach, so he scurried into some thick brush surrounded by cactus. From his vantage point he could see the cowboys and not be seen. Besides he knew they could not ride their horses into the thick cactus. They often knew of his presence, and they also knew he was armed. Their usual response was to yell at him and promise to catch him the next time, then ride off. His response always was to hide and try not to make any noise.

The ranch had some cattle roaming around eating the what grass they could find. The grass was so sparse it took many acres to support one cow, so on most hunting trips GA did not see a single bovine. Once he did come across a bull that took an instant dislike of him. It chased him up a tree, then spent a long time shaking the tree with its horns. It looked GA in the eye and bellowed at him. The tree was too stout for the bull to knock down but not large enough to allow GA to be comfortable. The bull repeatedly shook the tree then backed off as if to see what might have fallen out. Unlike the peccaries, the bull refused to give up and go away.

GA did not want to kill the animal, an act that would put an end to his hunting. He decided that he would shoot the bull in the horn to see if that would make him leave. He aimed very carefully while the bull was just below him. The bullet pierced the horn a few inches away from its head. He could see the small round hole appear in the horn. The bull fell to its front knees and made a loud noise expelling its breath and did not move for a while. GA feared that he had killed the animal, but after a while it stood up and staggered away in a daze. The bull did not die, but that experience ended GA's hunt for the day.

To get to the area of the ranch where he hunted, GA had to walk past the owner's home. One day the owner was on the porch, watching him. This made GA so nervous he let his pistol slip from under his jacket. The owner rushed over to GA and demanded to examine the pistol. He told GA that his fence riders had reported a young boy hunting with a pistol on his property, that every time they tried to approach him, he hid in the underbrush. The ranch owner knew much about GA, even that he was the Baptist preacher's oldest son.

GA admitted to being the hunter, explaining he was doing it only to keep his family from going hungry and that he hunted only rabbits and birds. Somehow it didn't seem necessary to mention the javelina incident. The rancher made GA come into his home. GA feared that he would call the police and take away the pistol. Instead the rancher explained that he did not allow anyone to hunt on his cattle ranch because it was too easy for a stray bullet to kill a cow, and cows were his livelihood. He went on to say that if GA would promise not to shoot any cattle, he could have permission to hunt on the ranch—but he had to limit his shooting to rabbits and birds for his family to eat and never shoot anything to sell. GA promised.

The rancher wrote a letter and signed it, giving GA special written permission to hunt on the ranch at any time. He told GA to just show the letter to any of his fence riders, and they would leave him alone. The surprised and happy GA never told the rancher that he had already shot a bull in the horn.

GA continued to hunt, and always carried the letter with him, but he still hid from the fence riders. Sometimes they would holler at him by name and sometimes ask him how his brothers and the preacher were—just to let GA know he was not fooling them. Then they always rode on and let him do his hunting.

Watch the Business

In 1930 GA had a friend who lived just across the border in Mexico. This friend's Dad had a business that was a combination grocery store, bar and casino. This was still during Prohibition so owning a bar just across the Mexican border had to be lucrative. The casino business consisted of card games, dominoes and a single slot machine that operated with quarters. GA's friend's job was to mind the business after lunch during the siesta time. No one ever showed up during his watch.

GA and his buddy, both curious sixteen-year old boys, put a lot of serious thought into how to beat the slot machine. They knew a young man that repaired slot machines, a fellow who said he could adjust the number of winning combinations on the wheels so the machine would either keep more or pay more, depending on how tight or loose the slot owner wanted. After the boys made friends with the slot mechanic, he gave them some options.

One was to purchase a coin he had soldered to a piano wire that was the perfect length to fool the slot machine. This would keep the coin from dropping into the machine and let you pull the handle repeatedly without additional coins. When you had won you simply pulled the wired coin out by the wire that kept it from falling all the way in, and you could use it again and again. The problem with this option was that some people had been caught with these devices. Most were severely beaten and some were even killed.

The boys wanted something that was less risky and faster. The slot mechanic gave them a suggestion that he thought might work, but he was not sure. The suggestion was to play the machine, and while the wheels were still spinning grab the machine, flip it upside down, then set it down, right side up.

They first tried it without the wheels spinning just to see if they could lift it. It was tough heave, and it took both of them to flip it over and set it back down. Nothing happened. Then they did it with the wheels spinning and the damned thing spit out all of its quarters.

They were delighted. They played this game every two or three weeks for some nice spending money. Then on the third milking of the slot machine, just as they had set it down and it was dumping out all its quarters, the friend's father walked in with a pistol in the hand.

The boys looked up at him in fear. He calmly said that he knew he was being robbed but he did not who was doing it or how until now. The man banned GA from the store, and he bolted the slot machine to a large counter so it could not be moved.

GA's friend was not allowed to associate with him on either side of the border anymore. All in all GA figured that they got off easy, considering that other slot machine thieves had ended up dead. His preacher father never found out about the theft.

Never Trust the Mail

In 1933 when president FDR established the Civilian Conservation Corps, GA signed up and spent a summer on Mount Graham near Safford, Arizona, in the Tree Army. The government paid GA $30 per month, sending $25 of it directly to his parents. But he didn't mind because he actually got to keep the other five, most of which he saved.

At one time GA had amassed the huge fortune for $20, which he put into an envelope and mailed to his parents. Somewhere in the postal system the envelope and money disappeared. GA regarded the theft as a bit of bad luck, but his work for the government left him with good memories for the rest of his life. The money his parents received helped them survive the Great Depression.

To put the tree army job into perspective, consider the job GA got after the Tree Army. It was shoveling gravel with a large square ended shovel for ten hours a day to earn one dollar. In this job there was no room for goofing off or resting: For those who could not keep up the pace, there were hundreds of unemployed men eager to take the job.

The Real Meaning of Hard Work

GA moved with his family to Corpus Christi, hoping to find work in a larger community. He found work on the docks as a longshoreman. GA was hired because he was old enough and because he was stronger than most other men. In those days there were no machines to pick up the two hundred pound sacks of sugar or flower or the "pigs" of lead. Longshoremen had to pick them up and carry them from the ship.

GA quickly discovered that the longshoremen had something in common with the grade school kids he once had to contend with. Longshoremen, too, had a pecking order, and a newcomer had to establish his strength ranking among the men. GA was rated fourth in strength of all the longshoremen because he could pick up 1,600 pounds of dead weight in lead pigs and tote it from the ship. Only three other longshoremen could lift and carry more. The strongest man could pick up and carry a 2,000-pound bale of cotton. These "adults," GA decided, were just older children, but at least they did not fight one another to establish the pecking order.

They did get drunk and sometimes fight, but it was just something to do when work was not available. The longshoremen had to work when the ship was in to be unloaded. They worked for four hours with a five-minute break every hour and got a half hour lunch break after the fourth hour. GA would do this for 24 hours, go home and sleep for twelve hours and return to do it again until the ship was empty. The men would then have some time off until the next ship arrived.

GA looked around for a better, way to make money. He found that he and one other strong longshoreman could dig a circular 30-foot deep cesspool three feet in diameter, brick it half way up and put a concrete lid on it—all in one twelve or thirteen hour day. When the hole they dug became too deep to pitch the dirt out, they rigged up a pulley with a five-gallon bucket. GA filled the bucket and his buddy, who was too big to fit in the hole, pulled up the bucket and emptied it. At the end of a long day, when the cesspool was complete, they could split thirty bucks for their labor. Word of mouth advertising kept them pretty busy.

Extortion is Just an Extension of Bullying

Years later, when GA set up his contracting business in Venezuela he made more money than he had ever made, which was necessary given that he had a wife, four children and many employees depending on him. Collecting the money proved to be a problem, for a while, but he took care of the problem.

Someone was delaying his checks, and he was not sure who or why. One day he went to pick up a check for work completed at the accounting office of one of the American oil companies. He had already made several trips for the check only to be told to come back later because the check required one more signature from a man who was not in to sign it. GA needed this check to pay his workers and payday was a couple of days away. He had to have that check.

The head of the accounting department met with GA and told him that he was the person that had the final approval on all his checks. He also said that GA would soon see how important the accountant was to GA's success as a contractor. It turned out this very important man wanted a patio added to a house he owned and expected GA to build it for free. When he explained the situation, he sat in a plush office chair looking up and GA with a smug smile.

A fit of rage enveloped GA. It was the same feeling he had over a red headed kid in the first grade a kid who seemed to be ruining his life thirty years before GA encountered the accountant. The red headed had been angry because he had to take the first grade over, so he struck GA. But the accountant was not mad. He just wanted a free patio for his mistress.

GA bent down grabbed the man by the collar, lifted him over his head, and slammed his back hard into the wall. He held the man by the neck against the wall with his left hand. He slapped him hard in the face five or six times alternately with his palm and then the back of his hand. When GA saw blood began to seep out of the man's nose, he let the man fall to the floor in a crumpled mess. The smug smile had turned into a look of shock and terror. When he touched his nose and looked at his fingers, he turned white at the sight of his own blood.

GA, speaking so everyone in the office could hear, told the man he would kill anyone who tried to extort money from him. Everyone in the office became quiet and turned to watch. GA said he was going out to his truck to get his shotgun and that his check had better be ready when he came back. He also told the man that he was a skilled hunter and that he would track him down anywhere in the country. If he tried to run and hide

GA would track him down.

As GA went out front to his pickup, people were quick to move out of his way. He got his shotgun from behind the front seat, waved it around in the air like a crazy man pretending he was shooting something, opened and closed the breech several times as if loading the gun, then waved the gun around some more as if he was shooting ducks or birds out of the sky. He made a show of replacing the gun in the truck and walked back into the building, heading straight for the accountant's desk.

A smiling woman intercepted GA. She called him by name and said that the man he was looking for had left for the day with a headache, but she had the check GA needed. GA took the check, politely thanked her, and left.

From then on when GA went to that office for his money, the same woman always greeted him, and she always had a friendly smile. She also had his checks ready like they were supposed to be. GA did not even have to say who he was or what he wanted; the checks were always ready. Rumor had it, GA heard, that the extortionist accountant suddenly retired and left the country, a rumor GA never verified, though he never saw that man again. He did take note that the approval signature on the checks became a different name. It matched the name plate on the desk of the woman with a smile.

Some key dates in GA's life

March 2, 1914 GA was born in Wagon Wheel Gap, OK, a town that no longer exists.

July 21, 1935 GA married a 17-year old beauty named Bell. We called her Mom.

July 22, 1936	Sue was born.
Jan. 24, 1938	Carl was born.
April 11, 1941	Jerry was born.
June 8, 1949	Gail was born.

GA died on December 11, 1986. When his children showed up for the funeral we were surprised to learn that GA had just converted and joined a church, the same church he had dismissed as a group of holy rollers. I immediately remembered a story Dad had told me about an old American Indian chief. He listened to the story the preacher told him and then he asked if it was really true that all he had to do was believe and he would be saved. The response was yes. He said that was good and that he had decided to wait until he was about to die and then believe, just in case. Meanwhile he continued to pray to the Great Spirit. I am sure GA died happy and content, whatever the meaning of his "conversion."

The True Word of God

Charlie Ritchie was a childhood friend of Dad's and a wonderful person. An airplane mechanic during World War II, he was shot up in some skirmish, a wound that resulted in his missing a yard or more of his intestines. He had to eat small amounts of food every two or three hours to keep from starving.

Dad got me a job working for Charlie in the summer of 1953 in Corpus Christi. I had just finished the ninth grade. Charlie made and sold trailers. He made the trailers using scrap metal he bought for three cents a pound and scrap lumber he scavenged mostly for the time it took him to pick it up and haul it away. My job was to help him build whatever trailer he was working on. Charlie allowed me to do anything except weld because Dad worried welding would be too hard on my eyes.

Charlie worked at a slow pace in order to build a trailer to his standard of perfection, and he had to stop every couple of hours to eat a snack. He never got in a hurry and hated deadlines, proclaiming that he had enough hurrying both in the military and being married, so he called a halt on ever hurrying again. He did strive for perfection and knew he could achieve his goals without rushing.

The first summer it took us three months to build two small trailers. My salary was five dollars per week. Dad supplied the five bucks and tried to conceal that from me, but it did not take long to detect the ruse. I tried not to let Dad I knew he came up with the weekly fiver. Mom gave me daily lunch money.

Charlie was a short man who had incredible strength. He could have been a gymnast in high school, for he had the build and the natural strength. He was also smarter than most people. Like Dad he could build anything with his hands, a talent that led him to being an outstanding airplane mechanic which in turn led to his belly being shot up pretty bad. When he healed from the wounds he stayed in the military as an airplane mechanic because he was so good at it and because there was a shortage of mechanics. Today the military would give a man with such a severe wound a total disability discharge and send him home.

After the war he became interested in woodcarving. He put together woodcarving kits with pre-shaped wood, a razor sharp carving knife, and directions for carving a wooden chain. The kit also had a starter block for carving a ball inside a wooden frame that would not come out of the cage. He packaged the kits in neatly labeled and designed cardboard boxes and tried his luck at selling them. They never made it as a big seller. One day when he was rummaging through one of his locked storage sheds he found a large box full of the kits, and he gave me several of them. They were a lot of fun.

Charlie lived in a house his mother had left him. It was a small, dirty old house that had not had a good cleaning since his mother died. The yard was full of scrap iron and scavenged lumber. Some of the scrap iron was future trailer parts and some just pieces of junk that interested Charlie. He knew where all the junk was and could tell me what future project he was going to use each pile for. We still made regular trips to the junkyard in search of some more treasures he could not live without. For him, collecting such junk was a kind of shopping addiction.

He picked out the scrap he wanted and paid his special rate of three cents a pound for it. Regular junkyard customers dealt in truckloads at a time, but Charlie rarely spent over a dollar. He usually told the cashier how much he thought it weighed and then pay for that weight without putting his treasures on the small scale. The cashiers would joke and threaten to bring out the magnet to be sure it was all iron. Sometimes he kept the smaller pieces hidden from sight in a burlap bag, and some-times he would put parts made of more expensive metals in the bag. He always joked with cashiers and talked to them about their families, and they often asked how many times he was going to pay three cents a pound for the old burlap bag. They knew what he was doing, but they never looked inside the bag or questioned his weight estimates because everybody liked Charlie. After I accompanied him on such a junk-buying trip, we drove to his house to add the new junk to his stacks of old junk. He rarely used any of his special scrap as parts to a trailer he and I worked on.

Charlie drove a 1946 Hudson pickup. The engine was a mess. He had driven it to Arizona in 1949 for a vacation to get away from people, to do some gold prospecting and to explore the last wilderness in the world, which he presumed was Arizona. Somewhere near Phoenix he ran into a haboob. He described it as a 30 mile wide wall of dust about 30,000 feet high. He drove in the dust until he could not see, so he pulled off the road and waited for it to pass. The storm filled everything with sand and dust.

He did not bother changing the oil, so sand in the oil ate up the rings in the engine. He never replaced the rings, though it would have been an easy job for him since he had the necessary tools and the ability to use them. He just did not want to do it because someone might expect it of him. Besides he was on vacation. He did not want to fit into any pattern of expected actions.

So he took his own kind of vacation to Arizona, which included driving many miles to the end of an old road. The road turned into a dirt trail and then into an open field. He parked near a ravine and walked a long way up to the ridge of an extinct volcano, sat on an old igneous rock to catch his breath and cherish the thought of possibly being the first white man ever to see the beautiful old volcano. He took a celebratory swig of cool water from his canteen, and as he lowered his head he noticed something shiny on the ground. He reached down between his legs and picked a brand new dime. The mint date was 1949.

This disappointing find spoiled his entire trip. He left Arizona and could not get back to Corpus Christi fast enough, convinced that the USA no longer had any unspoiled wilderness. He may have been right.

Because of the engine damage from the haboob sand, he took to carrying six quarts of cheap extra thick oil in the pickup to make sure the truck would get him home from a short trip like to the café for coffee and pineapple pie.

Charlie and I usually ate lunch in an old diner with a chrome-decorated counter top and round chrome stools with red cushions. Every time I go into a modern day "Five & Diner" restaurant I think of Charlie. The main differences are that today's "Five & Diner" counters are clean and the stools do not wobble. I would not sit on some of the stools the old diner because they were unstable.

On Wednesdays we tried to go to a different diner, a place that was known for its large bowl of great homemade beef stew. For a buck fifty you got a bowl with three chunks of beef, a large potato and lots of carrots. Coffee was a nickel. They always ran out of stew so you had to get there early. The stew was always served to a grungy looking bunch of skinny vagrants. We fit right in. Coffee refills were allowed but no stew refills were available. Someone always asked and even offered to pay extra only to be denied because the stew quickly sold out.

I never had enough money to leave a tip, but Charlie always

left something. If I ran out of cash Charley picked up my tab and wouldn't let me pay him back the next day. The stew place had other specials on other days, but Charlie never wanted to try them out. When we got there too late for the stew we left and went to the other diner for a cup of coffee and slice of pineapple pie. The price was two bits.

Charlie's father had been a holy roller preacher who spoke in tongues. Charlie had stopped going to this church when he was a teenager. Just before his death his father gathered his children around and told them that he had been a Rabbi, and they should have been raised Jewish. He had changed faiths to win over their mother. It turned out that in his waning years he had regretted his conversion . He told Charlie that as his oldest son Charlie should have been raised to be a Rabbi, and he was sorry about the vast education Charlie had missed. This left Charlie pretty confused about religion in general, but he tried to keep an open mind on the subject. His father died soon after that confession. His mother kept going to her church until she died a few years later.

One day some people set up a large tent across the street from where Charlie built trailers. They put up a large revival sign announcing "The True Word of GOD" would be presented daily for a week. That afternoon when Dad came to pick me up Charlie talked Dad into going with him to hear the woman preacher tell us the True Word of God. We went into the tent, down one of the many rows of wooden folding chairs, and joined the others for a few songs. They sounded like a revised version of some old Baptist Sunday school hymns I had heard. The hymnals were on the back of each chair. Those leading the singing even announced the next song by page number, just as did the Baptists, so the sound and feel of the service was just like the Baptist revivals I had gone to.

After some singing a red-headed woman in a robe came to the pulpit and said a prayer. She said she would lead us in prayer, but she did all the talking. Then she directed the ushers to pass the hat. The collection trays were straw baskets. Dad and Charlie each put in half a buck and since I was broke I just passed the basket on. The ushers took all the baskets to the red-headed woman, and she quickly counted the money.

She then spoke in angry tones, telling us that she wanted to thank the Lord for exactly twenty-two dollars and fifteen cents or something like that. I thought she looked too angry to pass as an ordained minister speaking from the pulpit. She told us that it took money to bring us the True Word of God and that she knew that there was at least one hundred dollars in this crowd of sinners. It seems her sermon could not be delivered before collecting at least that much money. After leading us in a moment of silent prayer that lasted about ten seconds, she directed the ushers to pass the hat again. She added that she would repeat this process as many times as it took until the sinners got it right.

This time when the basket came by it contained two shiny half dollars. Dad and Charley looked at each other and then at the basket. In quick moves and without saying a word they each retrieved their previous donation and passed the basket on to the surprised usher, and we left.

Sometime later the congregation must have gotten "it" right because we heard the red-headed woman droning out some message but we were too far away to distinguish exactly what her True Words of God were. We assumed we did not miss much. Charlie and Dad were too busy congratulating each other on how lucky they were to get their money back from the scam-artist preacher.

I worked two summers for Charlie. The second summer Dad raised my wages to ten bucks a week. It's a good thing that Mom supplied the money I spent on lunches. It was smart of Dad for setting this job up. I thank Mom, Dad and Charlie for the summer job, for it taught me much, kept me from being bored, and kept me too busy to get into any trouble. When I got home at night I was happy to get a bath, some food, and a good night's sleep.

The last trailer I helped Charley with was a special-order tandem job for some old rancher. Charley did not want to take the special offer, but the rancher doubled Charlie's original asking price. He wanted a sturdy trailer that would haul several steers at a time. The man even paid Charley extra to use new two by twelves for the flooring. The angle iron frames we bolted the flooring to were old bed frames Charlie had bought in the junkyard for three cents a pound. The steel bolts were also from the same source at the same price. They had been kind of rusty. Charley found them in a gallon bucket at the junkyard, and he stole them from the junkyard by putting then in his burlap bag. After Charley soaked them in some sort of fluid he put together that smelled like a mixture of kerosene and gasoline and I brushed them off with a steel wire brush, they looked as good as new. When they were bolted down and painted it was impossible to tell they had been junk. Charley said that the profits for that trailer would cover his living expenses for about a year. This made me happy.

Charlie died before I finished college. He could finally hear the True Word of God first hand. I still think he was a wonderful person. Having known him enriched my life.

Menhaden

In 1954 my family moved to Port Arthur, Texas. For a fun outing and a swim we often went to McFadden Beach, which was close to the road to Galveston. We would find a sandy path from the highway, then drive on the beach to park away from other people and spend the day.

The road from our home to the beach led us through two very smelly areas. The first was a series of oil refineries. The second was the Quinn Menhaden plant on Highway 87 between Port Arthur and Sabine Pass. The smell of the Menhaden plant was always the winner of the bad smelling award. The only good thing was that it did not take long to get past it. About all we knew about Menhaden was that it was used for fertilizer and it smelled worse than any cow lot or pulp mill.

In 1955 we moved to a nice rent house owned by the captain of a large menhaden fishing boat. Initially I got the impression that he also owned the menhaden boat, but this was probably not the case. In all likelihood he was only the captain, and the boat was part of a company fleet.

Menhaden are small oily, smelly fish with a lot of bones.

You probably could not force people to eat them fresh out of the water no matter how you prepared them. They are processed into meal, oil, and other components, which are then used in high protein food for chickens, turkeys, pigs, pets and cattle. Today if you consume Omega 3 to promote a healthier heart and reduce a high triglyceride level you are likely consuming menhaden.

The captain invited Dad and his two sons to go on a short fishing trip with him one Saturday. We got up early, and the captain drove us to the boat, a craft about 200 feet long. The crew had already loaded it with ice and fuel for the day. We went into the area of the Gulf of Mexico between Port Arthur and Galveston, cruising not far from the beach where we often went swimming. From the ship we could even see the Galveston highway with some traffic on it.

After a few hours of searching one of the company planes spotted a school of fish and radioed the location to the menhaden fleet. Our captain piloted the boat near the fish, and his crew encircled much of the school with hundreds of feet of net. The circle was about one hundred yards in diameter. The crew immediately started tightening the circle, making it smaller and smaller. When they started dipping the fish out of the circle we had drifted to within about two hundred yards of the beach.

The crew dumped the fish on the deck where a team of sorters separated the catch. They put the menhaden in the hold. The shark were piled on the deck, and the abundant cabbage head jellyfish were tossed over the side. The shark varied in size from a foot to over ten feet long. Some of the larger ones were hammerheads. After the fish were all captured, the crew cleaned the nets. The captain headed back to port. The crew unloaded the catch. The entire process was very well coordinated. Everyone knew his job and did it well at the exact right time without having to be told. What a great team they were.

While driving back home in his car the captain told Dad that the day's catch was worth about $32,000. To put this into perspective Dad was a union plumber. In 1954 he was given a dime an hour raise to $3.10 per hour, which meant his yearly income, at best, would be less than $6,000. We just did not comprehend the huge amount of money those fish were worth. We left the house at 6 AM and returned around 4 PM. Not a bad take for a ter-hour day. All it took was a large expensive boat, a large skilled crew, several spotter aircraft and a lot of coordinated hard work.

Menhaden fishing is still a big but declining industry from Alabama to Texas in the Gulf of Mexico. The boat crews now pump the fish from the net to the boat instead of the slower labor-intensive dip net process. The new pumping process now leaves time for the crew to catch more fish the spotter planes may have located. The decline in available menhaden these days appears to be due to over-fishing and to the increase in the number and kinds of jellyfish that compete for the same zooplankton the menhaden feed on. Like sardines there is not an endless supply of menhaden.

The Quinn Menhaden name was changed in 1990 to Daybrook Fisheries. Together Omega Protein and Daybrook fisheries catch on average about 1.2 billion pounds of menhaden per year in the Gulf of Mexico. Omega Protein was co-founded in 1953 by George Bush under a parent company called Zapata. Bush sold his interest in Zapata in 1966. Texas limits commercial menhaden fishing to a season that runs from the third Monday in April to Nov. 1.

It never occurred to me that one day I would be asked by my doctor to consume this smelly fish in the form of Omega 3 capsules for my health. The Omega 3 made from menhaden does not contain the levels of mercury found in other fish like tuna, salmon or mackerel.

My thanks to Doctor David S; he caused me to recall a fun teenage memory of the menhaden fishing trip.

Another Rosa

While living in the old Stadium Road house Mom hired a maid by the name of Rose, and—you guessed it. Mom called her *Rosa*. Rose was a squat, old African American woman with a protruding lower jaw or lantern jaw. The real problem that made her jaw protrude so much was her habit of constantly keeping her lower lip full of tobacco. She was a hard worker, a necessity to get everything done Mom gave her to do.

Mom noticed one day that something was gouging holes in her new linoleum flooring. She tracked it down to Rose who had a nail in the heel of one of her shoes. The nail had been blunted but still protruded enough to damage the flooring. Rose explained that the heel had fallen off her only pair of shoes so she nailed it to the sole. The nail was too long so she bent the end around and had tried to drive it into the heel, but part of it still protruded and gouged the floor. Mom gave her an old pair of tennis shoes one of us had outgrown, making the gift on the condition that Rose quit wearing the nail in the heel shoes in our house. She was thrilled.

Using oral tobacco was something Rose had done for many

years, and it became a serious problem. She loved it and was careful where she spit, if you can be careful about a thing like that. Shortly after starting to work for Mom Rose developed a malignant growth in her mouth The doctor who treated her had to take part of her lower lip when he removed the growth. She did not return to work after the surgery, and she only lived a few months more.

Small Time Betting

A bad bet

It was in the late 1950s working for a plumbing company when one really strong, fit-looking laborer in his late forties bet his entire weeks wages that he could lift three large brass valves with his teeth. Several adventurous co-workers covered the bet. The man strung a half-inch hemp rope thru the valves and left one lose end with a knot in it sticking out about a foot as a handle. His bet was that he could pick up the valves with his mouth and set them on a bench that was about waist-feet high. He grabbed the rope with some toothy fury and determination, strained—and the knot ripped out all of his front teeth leaving a bloody hole the size of the knot where his front upper and lower teeth had been.

Now that was a bad bet.

A Good Bet

The same plumbing company a few weeks earlier: a young plumber who was also a body builder bragged about how much stronger he was than everyone else. My Dad bet twenty dollars that he could lift a fitting box with all the cast iron fittings the body builder could lift plus the body builder and set both box and body builder on the waist-high bench.

The box was about six feet long, eighteen inches wide and two feet deep. It had a two inch steel pipe for a handle running down the middle. The body builder took the bet, and there was a lot of side bet action. The body builder put about six-hundred-pounds of fittings into the box. He made several trial runs, adding or removing fittings between trials. When he was finally satisfied with the weight and announced that this was it, he lifted the box to the bench with some difficulty. But he got it upon the bench. It took two of the side-betting plumbers to set the box of fittings back on the ground. The boastful body builder stepped into the fitting box with a smile and told Dad it was his turn. In a sudden burst of furious energy, Dad easily picked up the box and the surprised body builder, hoisted the weight about eighteen inches higher than necessary and dropped it on the bench. He collected his original bet and several side bets.

A few weeks later, Dad felt some responsibility for the toothless laborer. He said that if he had not been showing off to the body builder the man would not have risked his teeth with such a bet, so Dad helped the man with some of the dental bill.

Dad later said that he was never worried about lifting the toolbox. He had heard the bodybuilder say that he could lift over 600 pounds. Dad knew he could lift over 1,200 pounds It was a good bet for Dad.

Bets to Excess

One of the high schools where I taught had a coach who gambled. He carried several small note pads for keeping track of his numerous bets and was constantly soliciting wagers on any sporting event. He would wager on any high school, college or professional sporting event. It never seemed to occur to him that especially as a high school coach, such activity have legal, moral, or ethical ramifications.

Everyone in the community knew of his gambling. When asked about his constant gambling, his stock answer was to tell about his father, proclaiming that he must have inherited the habit from his father. When he was a teenager his dad lost their house and car on a high school football game wager. He said his mother would not speak to his dad for years after she had to move out of her home. The coach would say it must be a family tradition and addiction, then ask, "Do you want to place a bet?"

West Orange Junior High School

My first teaching job was for West Orange Junior High School, a middle school for sixth, seventh and eighth graders. Teachers were paid once per month; my annual salary was $3,750 per year, which was at the time above the State minimum wages for teachers. I was thankful to be hired by them. All the principals for the high schools where I had applied told me the same thing: go age some and come back in a few years. I looked younger than most of the students.

So I taught seventh grade math, science, social studies, arts and crafts, and home room. For home room I was an attendance monitor, money collector and tutor. The school was always having me collect money from the students for different things. Unfortunately, many of the parents made less than I did. A common occupation of my students' fathers was chipper. This job involved chipping rust from the bottoms of WWII ship that had been in storage for years.

The seventh grade teachers were supposed to teach almost everything to their home room class, but the school officials let us switch around and mostly teach our specialties. The usual social studies teacher liked to teach science, so I got to teach my home room group social studies and she taught science to her group. It was lucky for me (and the students) that another seventh grade teacher took my home room for English and I took her home room for Science because she did better with English than I could have.

One hour a day the students went to the high school for music or chorus. One day a week we devoted one hour to arts and crafts. As a color blind person, I did the best I could. I let them work on anything they wanted to so long as they stayed in their seats and remained quiet. I praised any and all completed art work. The class was mandatory but received no academic grade.

The high school, housed in a larger adjoining building, had a Biology teacher I knew. He and I graduated from the same high school, then four years later we were in the same college graduation class. He persuaded the School Superintendent to have a first annual high school biology field trip.

Most of the sophomore class and several teachers went to a local bayou and swamp area where they collected local flora and fauna. They brought back an assortment of things including samples of poison ivy (without knowing what it was), insects, lizards and a live grass snake. The busses loaded with students, teachers and the specimens returned during the last period of the day. The sophomore boy in charge of the grass snake put it in a large metal trash can similar to those that once stood by the exit door of every classroom in Texas.

The young man repeatedly picked up the grass snake to scare the girls, then dropped it back into the trash can. After being picked up and dropped thirty or forty times the snake took offense and bit the boy on the knuckle when he reached in one time beyond the snake's tolerance. It clamped down and did not want to let go. Because the bite didn't hurt much and because the boy knew the snake was not poisonous, he walked around the school from room to room holding out his hand with the attached snake. The new biology teacher had gone to assist with the unloading of the rest of the collected bounty.

One of the people the young man encountered was a first-year English teacher who hated snakes and thought all of them to be vile and deadly. To her credit she calmly pulled the student by his empty hand to the office.

In the office somehow the day's chaos really started. Within minutes there was an ambulance on the way, someone called the police, and if we had had a school nurse someone would have called the nurse. The new biology teacher showed up, but it was too late. He tried but could not calm the situation.

About this time in the Junior High School classes we were quietly studying and waiting for the school day to end. The multi-layer windows had been pushed open to catch any passing breeze. The school had heat for winter but no air conditioning, and it was a warm humid day. The social studies teacher that also liked to teach science was minding her home room group when a thirty-caliber bullet crashed through two plates of glass from the open windows, penetrated a metal strip of the Venetian blinds and knocked the surprised Chief of Police's seventh grade daughter out of her chair.

The teacher helped the girl up. One of the boys found the flattened spent bullet, which was still hot to the touch. The teacher had him set it on her desk for the police. Students notified the principal.

The girl had a hole in her dress about a half dollar in size and a bruise on her side just below the ribs. Someone called the police, and someone else called an ambulance. The ambulance people said that their only available ambulance was already on its way to the high school, and anyone needing it should go to the high school. A different ambulance service was called, a company that quickly dispatched an ambulance to the junior high. The secretary in the junior high's main office called the superintendent's office with the bad news but got a busy signal.

After the junior high principal ran to the high school to spread the news, the junior high office secretary remembered the girl's father was chief of police, so she called his direct line. Then she called the girl's mother at home.

In minutes an army of police entered both schools looking for a war. For a while there was a flurry of teachers, administrators, students and police running back and forth between the schools with panic on their faces.

Paramedics removed the snake from the boy's hand and euthanized it. The snakebite victim's trip to the hospital was delayed while officials debated transporting the gunshot victim with him. They couldn't call anyone for advice because the phone lines in both schools were jammed.

School officials finally decided against joint transport, and an ambulance departed with just the snake bite victim. The emergency staff in the hospital gave him a couple of shots and disinfected the small pricks that the snake's teeth had left on the knuckle.

The second ambulance with the girl had a police escort, so it beat the snake bite victim to the hospital. The girl's mother and father were waiting when her ambulance arrived. The Chief of Police's daughter was pronounced in shock but stable. She had only a silver dollar-sized bruise just below her ribs. The skin was not penetrated.

Police determined that the bullet was a 30.06 round and was most likely fired from a shooting range about five miles away. There was no record of anyone being at the range that afternoon. The range officer was off and the gates were locked. Back at the school, the maintenance crew repaired the windows.

But the Venetian Blind still had a hole in it the next School Year.

The poor snake was preserved in a bottle. The biology teacher affixed to the bottle a label giving the genus and species. Someone penciled in the sophomore's name it had bitten, but that was later erased.

The school did permit a second annual Sophomore Biology field trip, but the students were not allowed to collect snakes of any kind. Poison ivy was also off limits, given that several students and teachers had rashes from it. It contaminated students and teachers alike for several days after the trip because students were passing it around for close inspection when the new Biology teacher realized what they were passing around was not just weed. After it was determined to be the cause of all the new rashes it was disposed of. The janitorial staff probably used the same large trash can that held the snake when it was alive.

There was only one other event that my home room group found more exciting and thrilling. We had a roller skating party to celebrate the end of the school year, and being a good sport I actually put on a pair of skates for the first time. My second turn around the rink I stumbled and sailed head first into the metal bleachers and got a black eye.

The entire class saw it happen. They screamed for joy and applauded. I politely refused their many requests for an encore performance. Some wrote in their Annual that it was the best day of the school year.

Eighter from Decatur, County Seat of Wise

I took a job teaching Algebra in a North Texas town in 1964. Every day I would see a billboard as I drove from Denton to Decatur just as I came down a small hill and around a curve into Decatur. The billboard showed a large pair of dice rolled into a hard eight followed by the words "Eighter from Decatur County Seat of Wise."

The school was a beautiful old red brick building with a tile roof. But it was in sad need of repair: the tile roof was missing many of the tiles, the walls had holes in them, and many windows were missing glass. It was in a sad state of repair. My first day was a bad omen.

The school was filled with an invasion of crickets. The cleaning crew kept everyone out of the building while they swept dead crickets into two-foot high piles. The workers all wore white masks to help dull the stench of dead crickets and insecticide. They scooped them up into wheelbarrows with shovels that looked like they were designed to move large amounts of barnyard poop.

Workers pushed the wheelbarrows up a wide ramp and

emptied them in a couple of dump trucks. The two dump trucks were mostly full when they finally had scooped up all the crickets. The trucks departed and they opened all the doors and windows to let the bad smell out. Large fans were brought in the help freshen the air. The smell was mostly gone when we were finally allowed in the school.

I went to the office. The secretary walked in the door just ahead of me and her high heel shoe sank into and got stuck in a floor weakened by termites. She and I could not extract the shoe, so she called the maintenance engineer, a retired colonel. He cut the shoe out with a hammer and sharp chisel, leaving a hole in the floor. He said we had to wait until after lunch for the repair to be completed. I wondered what lunch had to do with it, but by being patient, I got an answer.

Meanwhile, he covered the hole in the floor with a chair and put a sign on the chair that said "DO NOT MOVE." Every student who came into the office had to move the chair and examine the hole in the floor.

After lunch he nailed an empty, flattened Vienna sausage can over the hole in the floor, a repair job that lasted as long as I taught there. Materials for repairs were in short supply and there was no budget, but fortunately we had a creative mainten-ance engineer.

That winter I got snowed on in the men's room as well as in my classroom. The students moved their desks around to keep the snow from falling on them. The desks were bolted to metal rails that had been screwed to the floor to keep the desks in line, but the floor had rotted out around the screws and the students had torn apart the metal rails so they could put the desks in dry places.

When drifts of snow started blowing into the room from a large hole in the wall near my desk I complained to the school secretary. The retired colonel arrived with a piece of plywood and a large rock. He put the plywood against the outside opening in the wall and used the rock to hold the plywood in place.

The custodian had to make three trips in the snow storm to make the repair. The first was to measure the hole, the second trip was to place the plywood over the hole—but the plywood blew down immediately. The third trip was to place a rock against the plywood big enough to hold it in place. The students gave him a round of applause.

He could not make all the radiators produce heat, but the snow quit blowing in through the wall. The students had already taken care of the snow coming through the ceiling by moving their desks around so it would not fall on them. We had several small piles of snow in random spots the classroom. We just walked around them.

Most of the roofing tiles were missing over the restrooms. The ceiling had been rained and snowed on so much that it had all fallen out. The only thing left were the rectangular metal frames that once had held the ceiling up, and many of them were bent or missing. Above the ceiling was what was left of a tile roof. There was no place to hang our coats, but that was not a problem. We had to keep them on to stay warm.

On the first day of school I met a young man about fourteen who stood almost five feet tall. He was not talkative, but his presence was hard to ignore because he had the body odor of a large sweaty mule. The PE coach said he had begged him to shower but could not convince him to use the free soap and towels the school provided. The Councilor told me that the highest the boy had ever scored on an IQ test was 65. The young man could print his name and chew tobacco, but he could not read, add, or subtract, and the only words he could spell were his name.

He was in my Algebra class because the school required Algebra for graduation. The principal explained that he was just one of a large family of more than fourteen children. He said he could not tell me how to grade the students. I told him that the boy could earn a D minus in my class by showing up and not causing any problems. D minus was the lowest passing grade in the school. The principal smiled and said that I understood some of the problem he faced every day. I moved the stinky student to a window seat in the back of the room, a window that was stuck open. When it snowed some of the other students helped him move out of the snow.

The third week of school his fifteen-year old sister showed up to take Algebra. Many of the students gathered around her before class and asked about her baby. Her mother was taking care of the baby while she was at school, but she had to go home several times during the day to nurse him. It did not seem to bother her that her milk flowed so much that her chest had wet spots about the size of saucers most of the time. From time to time she would get up and leave the classroom without saying a word.

I never asked her to tell me where she was going. I was afraid that she would tell me. Sometimes she returned right away and sometimes it was the next day or so. Unlike her brother she started every day with clean clothes and a bath. Sadly she dropped out of school before Thanksgiving. She was not married, though many said her baby looked a lot like one particular young man they knew. The father never claimed the child, and no one seemed to mind.

All my colleagues were hard working, dedicated teachers. I especially remember the Biology teacher, himself a graduate of Decatur high school, because he owned 50 head of Holstein milk cows. He said his vet bill for the milk cows exceeded his teaching salary, that he taught because he loved it.

I resigned just before Christmas vacation to take a better paying job. The Superintendent was furious with me for not completing the school year. He told me I better not ever come back looking for a job or a reference.

I never have.

Carl Craven has lived in villages, towns, and cities in Venezuela, Texas, Nevada, and Arizona. His father once traveled around Texas in a covered wagon and survived by hunting small animals on the Texas hardscrabble, a man who in the 1940s took his young family on a five-year adventure in Venezuela. Carl has earned his living as a construction worker, a math teacher, a computer programmer, a business executive, and a systems analyst. His passions have included salt water fishing, tennis, bowling, poker, hiking, and reading. He lives in Gilbert, Arizona, with his wife, Pat.